THE REVENGE OF CONSCIENCE

THE REVENGE
OF CONSCIENCE
Politics and the Fall of Man

J. BUDZISZEWSKI

Spence Publishing Company · Dallas
1999

Published in the United States by
Spence Publishing Company
111 Cole Street
Dallas, Texas 75207

Library of Congress Cataloging-in-Publication Data for the Hardcover Edition

Budziszewski, J., 1952–
     The revenge of conscience : politics and the fall of man / J.
Budziszewski.
        p. cm.
     Includes bibliographical references and index.
     ISBN 1-890626-16-3 (hardcover)
     1. Political Ethics.   2. Fall of man.   3. Sin, Original.   I. Title.
JA79.B832   1999
172—dc21   99-23511

ISBN 1-890626-27-9 (pbk.)

Printed in the United States of America

To Sandra, beyond rubies, best gift

In gratitude to the Maker

Blessed be He

Contents

Preface

EIGHTEEN YEARS AGO I stood before the Government Department of the University of Texas to give a talk. I was fresh out of graduate school, and it was my here's-why-you-should-hire-me lecture. I wanted to teach about ethics and politics, so as academic job seekers do everywhere, I was showing the faculty my stuff.

So what did I tell them? Two things. The first was that we human beings merely make up the difference between good and evil; the second was that we aren't responsible for what we do anyway. And I laid out a ten-year plan for rebuilding ethical and political theory on these two propositions.

Does that seem a good plan for getting a job teaching the young? Or does it seem a better plan for getting committed to the state mental hospital? Well, I wasn't committed to the state mental hospital, but I did get a job teaching the young.

My purpose, as a way of introducing this book, is to tell how I became a nihilist, and how I escaped from nihilism. Perhaps I should first explain just what my argument for nihilism was.

My two former claims have already been mentioned: that we

make up the difference between good and evil, and that we aren't responsible for what we do anyway. My argument reversed this order, because first I denied personal responsibility. The reasoning was not very original. We could not have free will, I thought, because everything we do or think or feel is just an effect of prior causes. It makes no difference that some of those prior causes are my previous deeds or thoughts or feelings, because those would be effects of still earlier causes, and if we traced the chain further and further back, sooner or later we would come to causes that are outside of me completely, such as my heredity and environment.

Second I concluded that if we have no free will, then good and evil cannot make sense. On the one hand I am not responsible for my deeds, so I cannot be praised or blamed for good or evil; on the other hand I am not responsible for my thoughts, so I cannot have any confidence that my reasoning will lead me to the truth about good and evil. So far it may seem that my argument was merely skeptical, not nihilist. But I reasoned that if the good for man cannot be known to man, then it cannot be offered to man as his good; for all practical purposes, then, there is no good.

This practical nihilism was linked with a practical atheism, for my arguments were couched in such a way that I thought they applied to God too. He couldn't escape causality either, I thought; therefore He couldn't possess confident knowledge of good and evil any more than I could. And even if He could achieve such a standard, it would make no sense for Him enforce it, because, entrapped in causality as He is, human beings have no ultimate control over their conduct. The upshot was that although God might exist, He would be irrelevant. I could not quite rule out the existence of God, but I thought I could rule out the existence of a God that mattered.

The holes in the preceding arguments are so large that one can see light through them. One hole is that in order to deny free will I assumed that I understood causality. That is foolish because I didn't know what causality really is any more than I understand what free will really is. They are equally wonderful and mysterious, so I had no business pretending to understand one in order to attack the other. Another problem is that my argument was self-referentially incoherent. If my lack of free will made my reasoning unreliable so I couldn't find out which ideas about good and evil are true, then by the same token I shouldn't have been able to find out which ideas about free will are true either. But in that case I had no business denying that I had free will in the first place.

At this point two things must be clearly understood. The first: One might think that my arguments for nihilism were what led me to become a nihilist, but that is not true. I was committed to nihilism already, and cooked up the arguments only to rationalize it. The second: One might think that my recognition of the holes in the arguments were what enabled me to *escape* nihilism, but that is not true either. I saw the holes in my arguments even at the time, and covered them over with elaborate nonsense like the need to take an ironic view of reality. Good and evil just had to be meaningless and personal responsibility just had to be nonexistent. The arguments were secondary. I was determined.

A friend—may he forgive me for quoting him—thinks my dismissal of my previous rationalizations as elaborate nonsense seems too pat. "Is it really that simple?" he asks. The answer is that, yes, it really is that simple. In my present opinion (though not my opinion of eighteen years ago), modern ethics is going about matters backwards. It assumes that the problem of human sin has to do mostly with the state of our knowledge; in other words, that we really don't know what's right and wrong and that we are trying to find out. Actually it has to do mostly with the state of our will. In other words, by and large we do know the basics of right and wrong but wish we didn't, and we are trying, for one reason or another, to keep ourselves in ignorance.

Is this an *ad hominem* argument—that because my motive was

bad, my nihilism must have been false? No, it is a diagnosis, with myself as case in point. My nihilism was *false* because it was self-referentially incoherent.* The motive was *bad* because although I knew this to be the case, rather than give up the nihilism I embraced the incoherency. What one must do with such a fellow is not to tell him what he doesn't know (because he really knows it), but to blow away the smokescreens by which he hides from the knowledge he has already.

Then how *did* I become a nihilist? Why *was* I so determined? What *were* my real motives?

There were quite a few. One was that having been caught up in the radical politics of the late 1960s and early 1970s, I had my own ideas about redeeming the world, ideas that were opposed to the Christian faith of my childhood. As I got further and further from God, I also got further and further from common sense about a great many other things, including moral law and personal responsibility.

That first reason for nihilism led to a second. By now I had committed certain sins that I didn't want to repent. Because the presence of God made me more and more uncomfortable, I began looking for reasons to believe that He didn't exist. It's a funny thing about us human beings: not many of us doubt God's existence and then start sinning. Most of us sin and then start doubting His existence.

A third reason for being a nihilist was simply that nihilism was taught to me. I may have been raised by Christian parents, but I had heard all through school that even the most basic ideas about good and evil are different in every society. That is empirically false—as C.S. Lewis remarked, cultures may disagree about whether

---

* There may exist nihilisms which are false for reasons other than self-referential incoherence, but I am speaking only of the version I held myself.

a man may have one wife or four, but all of them know about marriage; they may disagree about which actions are most courageous, but none of them rank cowardice as a virtue. But by the time I was taught the false anthropology of the times, I wanted very much to believe it.

A fourth reason, related to the last, was the very way I was taught to use language. My high school English teachers were determined to teach me the difference between what they called facts and what they called opinions, and I noticed that moral propositions were always included among the opinions. My college social science teachers were equally determined to teach me the difference between what they called facts and what they called *values,* and to much the same effect: the atomic weight of sodium was a fact, but the wrong of murder was not. I thought that to speak in this fashion was to be logical. Of course it had nothing to do with logic; it was merely nihilism itself, in disguise.

A fifth reason for nihilism was that disbelieving in God was a good way to get back at Him for the various things which predictably went wrong in my life after I had lost hold of Him. Now of course if God didn't exist then I couldn't get back at Him, so this may seem a strange sort of disbelief. But most disbelief is like that.

A sixth reason for nihilism was that I had come to confuse science with a certain world view, one which many science writers hold but that really has nothing to with science. I mean the view that nothing is real but matter. If nothing is real but matter, then there couldn't be such things as minds, moral law, or God, could there? After all, none of those are matter. Of course not even the properties of matter are matter, so after while it became hard to believe in matter itself. But by that time I was so disordered that I couldn't tell how disordered I was. I recognized that I had committed yet another incoherence, but I concluded that reality itself was incoherent, and that I was pretty clever to have figured this out—even more so, because in an incoherent world, *figuring* didn't make sense either.

A seventh and reinforcing reason for nihilism was that for all of the other reasons, I had fallen under the spell of the nineteenth-century German writer Friedrich Nietzsche. I was, if anything, more Nietzschean than he was. Whereas he thought that given the meaninglessness of things, nothing was left but to laugh or be silent, I recognized that not even laughter or silence was left. One had no reason to do or not do anything at all. This is a terrible thing to believe, but like Nietzsche, I imagined myself one of the few who could believe such things—who could walk the rocky heights where the air is thin and cold.

But the main reason I was a nihilist, the reason that tied all these other reasons together, was sheer, mulish pride. I didn't want God to be God; I wanted J. Budziszewski to be God. I see that now. But I didn't see it then.

I have already said that everything goes wrong without God. This is true even of the good things He's given us, such as our minds. One of the good things I've been given is a stronger than average mind. I don't make the observation to boast; human beings are given diverse gifts to serve Him in diverse ways. Besides, no one will suppose that a person gets into a scholarly career by accident. The problem is that a strong mind that refuses the call to serve God has its own way of going wrong. When some people flee from God they rob and kill. When others flee from God they do a lot of drugs and have a lot of sex. When I fled from God I didn't do any of those things; my way of fleeing was to get stupid. Though it always comes as a surprise to intellectuals, there are some forms of stupidity that one must be highly intelligent and educated to commit. God keeps them in his arsenal to pull down mulish pride, and I discovered them all. That is how I ended up doing a doctoral dissertation to prove that we make up the difference between good and evil and that we aren't responsible for what we do. I remember now that I even taught these things to students; now *that's* sin.

It was also agony. You cannot imagine what a person has to do to himself—well, if you are like I was, maybe you can—what a person has to do to himself to go on believing such nonsense. St. Paul said that the knowledge of God's law is "written on our hearts, our consciences also bearing witness." The way natural law thinkers put this is to say that they constitute the deep structure of our minds. That means that so long as we have minds, we *can't not know* them. Well, I was unusually determined not to know them; therefore I had to destroy my mind. I resisted the temptation to believe in good with as much energy as some saints resist the temptation to neglect doing good. For instance, I loved my wife and children, but I was determined to regard this love as merely a subjective preference with no real and objective value. Think what this did to the very capacity to love them. After all, love is a commitment of the will to the true good of another person, and how can one's will be committed to the true good of another person if he denies the reality of good, denies the reality of persons, and denies that his commitments are in his control?

Visualize a man opening up the access panels of his mind and pulling out all the components that have God's image stamped on them. The problem is that they all have God's image stamped on them, so the man can never stop. No matter how much he pulls out, there's still more to pull. I was that man. Because I pulled out more and more, there was less and less that I could think about. But because there was less and less that I could think about, I thought I was becoming more and more focused. Because I believed things that filled me with dread, I thought I was smarter and braver than the people who didn't believe them. I thought I saw an emptiness at the heart of the universe that was hidden from their foolish eyes. Of course I was the fool.

How then did God bring me back? I came, over time, to feel a greater and greater horror about myself. Not exactly a feeling of guilt, not exactly a feeling of shame, just horror: an overpowering *true intuition* that my condition was terribly wrong. Finally it occurred to me to wonder why, if there was no difference between the wonderful and the horrible, I *should* feel horror. In letting that thought through, my mental censors blundered. You see, in order to take the sense of horror seriously—and by now I couldn't help doing so—I had to admit that there was a difference between the wonderful and the horrible after all. For once my philosophical training did me some good, because I knew that if there existed a horrible, there had to exist a wonderful of which the horrible was the absence. So my walls of self-deception collapsed all at once.

At this point I became aware again of the Savior whom I had deserted in my twenties. Astonishingly, though I had abandoned Him, He had never abandoned me. I now believe He was just in time. There is a point of no return, and I was almost there. I said I had been pulling out one component after another, and I had nearly got, shall we say, to the motherboard.

The next few years after my conversion were like being in a dark attic where I had been for a long time, but in which shutter after shutter was being thrown back so that great shafts of light began to stream in and illuminate the dusty corners. I recovered whole memories, whole feelings, whole ways of understanding that I had blocked out.

Of course I had to repudiate my dissertation. At the time I thought my career was over because I couldn't possibly retool, rethink, and get anything written and published before my tenure review came up, but by God's grace that turned out to be untrue.

What I do now as an ethical and political theorist is poles apart from what I did eighteen years ago. What I write about now is those very moral principles I used to deny—the ones we *can't not know* because they are imprinted on our minds, inscribed upon our consciences, written on our hearts.

Some call these principles the "natural law." Such as it is, my own contribution to the theory of natural law is a little different from those of some other writers. One might say that I specialize in understanding the ways that we pretend we don't know what we really do—the ways we suppress our knowledge, the ways we hold it down, the ways we deceive ourselves and others. I do not try to "prove" the natural law as though one could prove that by which all else is proved; I do try to show that in order to get anywhere at all, the philosophies of denial must always at some point assume the very first principles they deny.

It is a matter of awe to me that God has permitted me to make any contribution at all. His promise is that if only the rebel turns to Jesus Christ in repentant faith, giving up his claims of self-ownership and allowing this Christ the run of the house, He will redeem everything there is in it. Just so, it was through my rescue from self-deception that I learned about self-deception. He has redeemed even my nihilist past and put it to use.

Many of my students tell me they struggle with the same dark influences that I once did. It is more difficult for a colleague to make such a confession, but some of them have also spoken to me. They describe the temptation as a kind of gravitational force, pulling them into darkness. I hope that by telling the story of my own escape I may encourage them to see and seek the light of the Redeemer, the God of truth.

THIS KIND OF BOOK comes together in bits and pieces, passing through many hands over a long period of time. To Mitchell Muncy, editor in chief of Spence Publishing, I am grateful for steady support and consistent good advice. The preface of this book began life as an invited talk but has been reprinted in both *Real Issue* and *Re:Generation Quarterly*. Several paragraphs of chapters two and nine first appeared in the *Human Life Review*, and an anecdote or two in *Citizen,* but the earliest complete version of chapter two was first written at the invitation of Mr. William Gairdner for the anthology *After Liberalism* (Stoddart, 1998). From my earlier work *True Tolerance* (Transaction, 1992) I have also borrowed a few paragraphs for chapter three, but the chapter attained its present form as an address to a group of graduate students at Yale University, at the invitation of Professor Steven Smith. Another address formed the embryo of chapter nine—an inaugural "charge" to the Paul B. Henry Institute for the Study of Christianity and Politics at Calvin College, which I was summoned to present by Professor Corwin Smidt. To my friend W. Bradford Wilcox, I owe the spur for chapter five. Professor Stanley Hauerwas has encouraged the project, and I owe him the further debt of a turn of phrase which I am sure he will recognize. The Reverend Christopher Hancock is responsible for prompting me to think about smokescreens, although he bears no responsibility for the direction in which I have taken the idea. The Reverend Peter Leithart, who thinks I cannot possibly believe *both* in depravity *and* in the natural law, has offered indispensable criticism of some of my claims about general moral revelation. To Mrs. Donna Ware and others, my thanks for sharing insights about the psychology of abortion. Versions of chapters two through seven have appeared in *First Things,* the monthly journal of religion and public life, to whose editors I am deeply grateful. Father Richard John Neuhaus, its editor in chief, must have been the only person in North America to have read a certain piece of my work which would otherwise have vanished into oblivion; without his invitation to contribute to the magazine, a good portion of this book might never have taken shape. My wife, Sandra, a profoundly gifted crisis pregnancy counselor, has stirred and disturbed my thinking by her conversation in ways which I cannot begin to analyze and acknowledge; I would call this book a partnership, were it not that this incomparable helpmate might then be blamed for whatever stupidities it may yet contain. To others who cannot be named I also give deep thanks, and to many who could be named, were it not for the frailty of memory. At last I speak my gratitude to Him to whom all hearts are open, all desires known, and from Whom no secrets are hid. May He cleanse the words of this book, as He cleanses the words of our praise.

THE REVENGE OF CONSCIENCE

Laws politic, ordained for external order and regiment among men, are never framed as they should be, unless presuming the will of man to be inwardly obstinate, rebellious, and averse from all obedience unto the sacred laws of his nature; in a word, unless presuming man to be in regard of his depraved mind little better than a wild beast, they do accordingly provide notwithstanding so to frame his outward actions, that they be no hindrance unto the common good for which societies are instituted: unless they do this, they are not perfect. It resteth therefore that we consider how nature findeth out such laws of government as serve to direct even nature depraved to a right end.

Richard Hooker

It is, therefore, a just political maxim that every man must be supposed a knave, though at the same time it appears somewhat strange that a maxim should be true in politics which is false in fact.

David Hume

I

The Fallen City
(apologion)

THIS BOOK IS A CHRISTIAN REFLECTION on the theme of politics and original sin. Simply put, I want to talk about what
it means to our common life that we are "fallen." Fallenness
is a paradox: We are neither simply good nor simply bad, but created
good and broken. We are not a sheer ugliness, nothing so plain, but
a beauty ruined.

Numerous objections are raised to such books, and I have heard
most of them. The bluntest is that anyone who speaks of politics
must impersonate an atheist. This complaint first reached me as a
new-minted scholar, just escaped from atheism myself, when a re-
viewer recommended against the publication of one of my early efforts
on grounds that "God does not belong in political theory." Paradoxically, he liked the book, but objected on principle to the mention of God. There is no point trying to reason with such people;
this one went on to blame me, more or less, for the massacre of the
Huguenots in 1572. I have forgiven him, but he still interests me. If
I am to blame for the religious butcheries of the sixteenth century, is
he to blame for the secular savageries of the twentieth? I see your
thousand Frenchmen; I raise you a million Chinese.

5

Of course the demand to impersonate atheists is not confined to the humane studies; scientists suffer it too. Indeed, biologist Richard Lewontin of Harvard proposes more than impersonation.

> Our willingness to accept scientific claims that are against common sense is the key to an understanding of the real struggle between science and the supernatural. We take the side of science *in spite of* the patent absurdity of some of its constructs, *in spite of* its failure to fulfill many of its extravagant promises of health and life, *in spite of* the tolerance of the scientific community for unsubstantiated just-so stories, because we have a prior commitment, a commitment to materialism. It is not that the methods and institutions of science somehow compel us to accept a material explanation of the phenomenal world but, on the contrary, that we are forced by our a priori adherence to material causes to create an apparatus of investigation and a set of concepts that produce material explanations, no matter how counterintuitive, no matter how mystifying to the uninitiated. Moreover that materialism is absolute for we cannot allow a divine foot in the door.*

The significance of such a remarkable confession is that we have been using the name "fundamentalist" for the wrong people. These days it is the theists who want to follow the evidence and the materialists who want to ignore it.

But let us leave the sciences and return to the study of man. A more thoughtful objection to a book like this, worth lengthier examination, comes from a colleague who worries about the cacophony of voices in the modern world. He says there are *too many* religions, *too many* philosophies, *too many* sacred texts. We are in a new and unprecedented intellectual condition, he tells me—a Pluralism. Understand that he is not a relativist; it would be impossible to rate

---

  * Richard Lewontin, "Billions and Billions of Demons," *New York Review of Books,* January 9, 1996.

too highly the persistence with which my friend seeks absolute values in this Babel. My disagreement begins with his description of the Babel as new. After all, the Tower of Babel is a very ancient tale, and just as many voices, sects, and doctrines quarrelled in premodern times as today. Nor were the thinkers of those times deaf to all the racket. Augustine contended with Gnostics, Platonists, Jews, Stoics, and Epicureans, among others; Maimonides wrote a *Guide for the Perplexed*; Thomas Aquinas cast his *Summa Theologiae* in the form of disputed questions. Babel, I suggest, is not a modern revolution, but the enduring condition of the fallen human race.

The Illusion of Neutrality

Even so, there is something new in the *manner* in which my friend and other moderns respond to Babel. It is not surprising that some thinkers deny absolute values; in one form or another, relativists, sophists, and skeptics have been with us from the beginning. Nor is it strange that others affirm them; in most eras the relativists, sophists, and skeptics have been in the minority. The novelty lies the *way* in which moderns affirm them when they do. Let me contrast their way, which my friend and most scholars call Pluralist, with an older way, which I will call Classical.

All those who practice the Classical way of affirming absolute values have two things in common. If you will pardon the coinages, they are all apologetical, and they are all noetic. By calling them apologetical, after the Greek word for "a speech in defense," I mean that each stakes a claim and defends it. Each makes some one voice in the Babel his own, then takes on his competitors by arguing the issues on their merits. The Epicurean tells you *why* he thinks pleasure the sovereign good; the Christian tells you *why* he thinks Jesus the risen son of God; the Gnostic tells you *why* he thinks evil coeval with good. And by calling them noetic, after the Greek word for "knowledge or understanding," I mean that their arguments appeal to shared knowledge rather than shared ignorance. Aristotle begins every ethical discussion with what almost all men in almost all times and places have believed. St. Paul, who quotes poets to pagans, says that God has not left Himself without a witness even among the nations: He has written His law on the heart. Thomas Aquinas holds that there are certain moral principles we can't not know—principles that do not have to be proved because they are what everything is proved from. C.S. Lewis dares his readers to "Think of a country where people were *admired* for running away in battle, or where a man felt *proud* for double-crossing all the people who had been kindest to him. You might just as well try to imagine a country where two and two made five." Even Wittgenstein nods in the noetic direction when he calls philosophy an "assembling of reminders" rather than a discovering of things that have never been noticed.

Notice that because a Classical affirmer is noetic, he does not take the Babel around him quite at face value. He will say that if I seem completely ignorant of a basic moral precept, the reason is less likely to be that I really do not know it, than that I do not want to know it and am holding my guilty knowledge down. Moreover, the Classical affirmer will regard an age like our own, in which even the most basic moral precepts are widely and increasingly denied, as exceptional even for this broken world. Before too long, any culture in deep moral denial must come to its senses or collapse, for the consequences of denying first principles are cumulative and inescapable.

By contrast with the Classical way of affirming absolute values, the Pluralist way is *anoetic* and *anapologetical.* Pluralists are anoetic because they *do* take the Babel around them at face value. Their arguments appeal to shared ignorance rather than shared knowledge. So far as we know, they say, every religion and every philosophy is equally in the dark and equally in the light. Although Pluralists may well agree that our age is exceptional rather than typical, they see this not as an omen of corruption but as a portent of an impending forward leap—a sign that our old philosophies have exhausted

themselves and we need to try something new. What is the something new? This is where being anapologetical comes in. The Pluralist *denies* the need to make one voice in the Babel his own; he
refuses to stake out a position, then argue its claims on their merits.
By adopting a posture of neutrality among competing goals and aspirations, of equal concern and respect for them all (that becomes
one of his absolutes), he tries to escape the futility of interminable
apologetics and carve out a new moral sphere in which people of
every point of view can get along: sodomists with socialists, pickpockets with Platonists, hedonists with *Hassidim*.

   This is a serious enterprise, and we ought to treat it as such. In
the meantime notice its implications. In his own way, the Pluralist
too thinks "God does not belong in political theory." He does not
object to Christianity as a *mistaken* point of view; disputing its claims
would be too crude. Rather he objects to it as a *point of view*—just
one more of the pullulating things, down there among the Platonists
and pickpockets. Pluralism floats chastely above them, out-topping
knowledge by the sheer force of nescience: "Others abide thy question; I am free."

   In fact, Pluralism does not float above them, but only seems to.
Is there a way to have equal concern and respect for the views of
both the rapist and the woman he wants to rape? Of course not.
Either he gets his way, or she gets hers. Admitting this, some Pluralists try to defend the ideal of equal respect as merely a starting
rather than an ending point. For example they say that the rapist
may be thwarted because he has already broken the symmetry: she
respects his plans, but he does not respect hers. Alas, this does not
work. It is a part of her plan that men in the neighborhood comply
with her ideas of proper male behavior no less than it is a part of his
plan that women in it comply with his ideas of proper female behavior. The true reason we call his plan wicked but not hers is that we
already know that rape is wrong; in other words, we know that her
aspiration for men and women to act like gentlefolk is good, whereas

his aspiration for them to act like animals is bad. Neutrality is not our starting- any more than our ending-point. The Pluralist only lets in by the back door what he has thrown out the front.

Fooling ourselves about our starting-points might not be so bad if we always wound up where we ought to be, but that is not what happens in Pluralism either. My colleague thinks reasonable people of all persuasions will agree that since we do not know whether the fetus is a human being, we should let each woman decide for herself whether to have an abortion or not. There is the argument from ignorance again. But even if it were true that we do not know what babies are—a point I do not concede—why should we say that because the baby might not be human we may kill him? Why not say that because he might be, we should protect him? We do not say that because I might not hit anyone, I may swing my hatchet blindly in a crowded room; we say that because I might hit someone, I shouldn't. Besides, it is a little thin to claim certainty that humans have surpassing value, yet ignorance about whether our own young are human—to flaunt our wisdom about the *what* of being human, yet deny having any about the *who*.

What we see then is that no decision is ever neutral, and Pluralism functions merely as a license to be arbitrary. While claiming to reconcile competing views without deciding which is true, it covertly supposes the truth of one of them but spares itself the trouble of demonstration. What this suggests is that the Classical way of affirming absolute values has more going for it than the Pluralists concede. Certainly it has more integrity. Maybe we should *not* take the surrounding Babel at face value; maybe we *should* go back to apologetics. If we are serious, we might even consider Christianity.

THE FALL OF MAN

Very well, Christianity. But why original sin? Because the three great troubles of public life are all results of the Fall. Politics would have been easy in Eden, but that was a long time ago. One of our troubles is plain and practical: we do wrong. The second is intellectual: we not only misbehave but misthink, not only do wrong but call it right. The third, of course, is strategic, for the second affects our efforts to cope with the first. Our toils to rectify sin are themselves twisted by sin, our labors to shed light on iniquity themselves darkened by iniquity. No mind is unstained, no motive unmixed. We cannot fix ourselves. We might as well expect a surgeon to sew his severed hands back on.

There is one hope. But because one of the greatest and deepest temptations of politics is to identify it prematurely, allow me to do that which would otherwise, for the pain of it, be inexcusable—to speak a bit longer of the malady, and of how we think about it.

Most political ideologies just deny it. In America, the most prevalent ignore it. There is the progressivism which thinks that if only the citizens would stand aside, government would fix everything. Then there is the libertarianism which thinks that if only the government would stand aside, the market would fix everything. On the one hand is the hubris of the experts, whose war against poverty multiplied poverty and whose tender care for the common man erected an imperium of judges and bureaucrats. On the other hand is the cupidity of the amateurs, for in the marketplace our desires are aroused so assiduously and scratched so efficiently that we spend our lives and fortunes just finding new places where we might itch.

The universities are dominated by ideologies of another kind: smarter in one way, but stupider in another. How are they smarter? They misidentify the deeper problem of original sin, but at least they are looking for a deeper problem. Marxists locate it in ancient class conflict, feminists trace it to primordial war between the sexes, but both see blindness and cruelty as inevitable, on grounds that everything a person thinks and seeks is determined by his class or sexual interests. How then are these ideologies stupider? Because if they are right, they indict themselves. The marxism of the marxist must be determined by *his* class interests, and the feminism of the feminist by *her* sexual interests. If their theories are right, then inevitably they will be as blind and cruel as their counterparts. The only way they can escape the dilemma is to declare themselves the sole exception to their theories. Left-leaning academics, technocrats, feminists must claim that *they* somehow *can* rise above their class and sexual interests—or that even though they cannot, it will be all right, because these momentary personal interests just happen to coincide with the long-range universal interests of the whole human race.

Then there is the ideological fashion called postmodernism—smarter yet, but stupider yet. How is it smarter yet? It recognizes that ideologies like marxism and feminism are hoist with their own petard, laughs, and claims to be "suspicious of metanarratives"—which means suspicious of *other people's* ideologies. As feminists and marxists claim to rise above the fairy tales of men and capitalists to achieve the truth, so postmodernists claim to rise above the fairy tales of feminists and marxists to achieve the insight that there is no truth. There is no "how the world really is," they say, only a struggle over who gets to say "how the world really is." How then is this stupider yet? Because it is still a story of how the world really is—a story of a struggle over who gets to tell the story. Those who boast of their suspicion of metanarratives are merely offering a meta-metanarrative—worse yet, a meta-metanarrative in denial, an ideology about ideologies which denies being an ideology. I hope it is plain who gets the benefit of the *meta-meta*. If chattering is all there is, then the chattering classes rule.

I said earlier that there is hope. It may seem that there could be none. To say we cannot fix ourselves—that we are like surgeons with severed hands—isn't that to admit as much? But if the surgeon's hands are severed, it follows only that another surgeon must mend him. Therefore reason does not preclude all hope; rather it precludes all hopes but one. Cure, if it comes, must come from God.

Standing outside our class interests, sexual interests, and all other broken interests, only He is in a position to heal. We cannot even reach Him, but He can reach us.

That brings us to yet another kind of objection, and the murmurs well up even before the details of salvation are announced. One voice asks, "To which god or prophet do you propose that we turn? Shall we follow Moses or Jesus, Muhammed or Krishna, Siddhartha Gautama Buddha or Diana of the Ephesians?" Another asks, "If we are too far gone in sin to save ourselves, then why aren't we too far gone to recognize the Savior? How can we know that faith is not just another sinful delusion?" A third wants to know, "Even if Jesus is who He said He was, we remain who He said we are. Wouldn't our supposed addiction to selfish interests merely pervert his movement into another tool of someone's injustice to someone else?" Demands the fourth, "Why are we talking about politics anyway? Didn't this Jesus say that his kingdom was not of this world? His was not the way of laws and legislatures, but of the Cross."

The first objection is misconceived, because the various religions offer different things. Diana was not interested in fixing us. Krishna and Siddhartha wanted to fix a different problem. Muhammed supposed that we *could* fix ourselves. Moses gave us the law of God which shows the true nature of the problem, but he did not give us power to follow it. For that, he looked to the Messiah yet to come, and according to Christianity, that Messiah was Jesus. He is not parallel to any of the others. Only He claimed not to *teach* but to *be* the surgery of God. "He was wounded for our transgressions, he was bruised for our iniquities; upon him was the chastisement that made us whole, and with his stripes we are healed" (Isa. 53:5, RSV).

As to the second: Yes, of course. The Christian faith holds that we *are* too far gone to recognize the Savior by ourselves. Faith is a gift. Only the God who sent Him could enable us to recognize Him. We do not "rise above" our selfish interests; we cooperate as Christ works in us to demolish them.

As to the third: Yes, again. The Christian scriptures not only admit that the faith can be corrupted, they predict that it will be. And so it often has been. The whole point about sin is that you get the worst things by taking the best things and perverting them. That is why the Church is warned that lies and delusions will be spread in the name of the truth—but it is also promised divine help to see through them, such help that the gates of death will not prevail against it.

And as to the fourth: Yes, to turn the gospel into a party platform is to pervert it. God saves; parties do not. That is exactly why this book is about politics and *sin*. But how does it follow that my party platform should be protected from the influence of the gospel? If even when I sweep the floor I should sweep it "as unto the Lord," then surely the Lord will not be indifferent to what I say in the public square. Scripture does not supply a ten-point political program; nevertheless it supplies a point of vantage from which every ten-point program can be called to judgment. St. Paul said "We destroy arguments and every proud obstacle to the knowledge of God" (2 Cor. 10:5).

In that sense there can be such a thing as a Christian political philosophy. It is a work of preserving grace, not saving grace, and like salt, it preserves by stinging. It is a perpetually unfinished work, because it stands in need of the very salt it strews. But it dares not stop stinging until Christ returns and the world is made anew.

EXPLAINING OURSELVES

Very well, original sin. But what can one say about it beyond the fact that we are Not Nice? And how does that explain anything?

I have already explained that there is much more to original sin than being Not Nice. That was the point of the opening paragraph about paradox—that we are neither simply good nor simply bad, but created good and broken. The aim of our reflection should be to find out how "created good and broken" is *different* from "simply good" and "simply bad," for the paradox dwells in every room of our house. Consider conscience. By and large we know when we do wrong, but will we admit to ourselves that we know? A law is written on the heart, yet we suppress it. What can we say about that? Depraved conscience turns out to be as different from genuine ignorance as it is from honest recognition—a point which tends to be overlooked by both the advocates and the critics of the notion of natural law. It is not a midpoint, but a third thing altogether.

In the title chapter, *The Revenge of Conscience,* I argue that recovering this biblical insight makes it possible to explain a number of things about our present social collapse that are otherwise unfathomable: in particular, why we decay so quickly. The usual explanation is that conscience is merely a restraint against our sinful desires, that it comes from socialization, and that it is weakened by neglect. However, this story cannot account for the sucking and dragging force of evil—how, like a bog, it draws us ever deeper in—how we invent ever new ways of doing wrong that seem to turn our desires inside out. We sin not only in pursuit of desire but in the teeth of desire. Conscience depraved is a much more complicated and dangerous thing than we suppose.

The third chapter, *The Illusion of Moral Neutrality,* considers not original sin in itself but one of its ideological outworks. We have scaled this outwork once before, in my earlier comments on Pluralism; here the object is to dig underneath and undermine it, which takes a little longer. Neutrality is the idea that we can choose how to live together while somehow avoiding commitment to a view of how things are. This idea is rich in benefits. In the final analysis it is a way of escaping responsibility—our time's variation on "The woman you gave me, she gave me the fruit." But it has other advantages too. It gives us something to say when we have nothing to say. It puts opponents on the defensive by defining opposition itself as "bias." And it is incoherent. If we had been educated properly we would consider this last as something bad; in times like ours it is viewed as something good, because from a logical inconsistency you can get anywhere. P *and* not-P implies any Q you like. For this reason neutrality will sleep with anyone, and that is why it turns up in so many places in this book: not only in the third chapter, which focuses on how it masquerades as tolerance, but more briefly in three others.

Chapter four is *Politics of Virtues, Government of Knaves.* I commented earlier that the three great troubles of public life are all results of the Fall: We do wrong, we think wrong, and the second trouble makes the first one worse. This chapter reflects upon how our inability to fix ourselves applies to the design of our political institutions. How can we make government promote the common good when there is so little virtue to be found? If we cannot fix original sin, can we somehow get around it? Is there a way to make that little bit of virtue go farther, to get more miles to the gallon? The framers of our own republic thought there was. Their boast was a New Science of Politics which would establish a New Order for the Ages. Yet the institutions of their *novus ordo seclorum* work quite differently than they expected. Consider just the innovation of making the Constitution a written law enforceable in courts: Their intention was to fortify the durable will of the people against the transient will of the people, but the effect was to enthrone the transient will of a judicial elite, which in time came to realize its power. This chapter takes a longer view. Over the ages, human thought has devised a sevenfold repertory of ways to "get around" what it cannot fix: Deterrence, Filtration, Compensation, Balance, Channeling, Inculcation, and Subsidiarity. The purpose of this chapter is to weigh what each one can and cannot do.

The next three chapters do double duty. If the doctrine of the Fall is true, then we should expect every worldly ideology to be scarred by moral error and self-deception. One of the purposes of the trio, then, is to root these fallacies up. But if the transformation of the mind is laborious and slow, then Christians must be on guard against falling back into the same errors themselves, confusing the delusions of their culture with the teachings of the faith. My other purpose, then, is to sharpen the contrast. Foundational to this effort is chapter five, *The Problem With Communitarianism*.

Communitarianism is the intellectual movement which tries to find "common ground" between liberals and conservatives in the notion of shared community values. That raises two questions: which community we share, and where its values come from. Complicating the first question is that Christians are members of two cities, the heavenly and the earthly, and the former is both higher and more encompassing than the latter. Complicating the second question is that a value can be communally shared without being good. One possibility is to fall back on the values that all communities embrace, but no such values exist. Another possibility is to fall back on the ones that all communities *ought* to embrace because God has written His law on our hearts. Here the problem is different; some traditions maintain strongly the reality of this "general" revelation, while others deny it. Paradoxically, then, even the appeal to the universal presupposes the particular; for insight into what we hold in common, we must fall back on traditions we do not hold in common.

The failure of communitarianism brings us to the other two *Problem* chapters, which concern the more familiar intellectual movements liberalism and conservatism. As I think of them my mind returns to a prayer of invocation at a political party convention which I attended as a delegate. There would have been nothing wrong in asking for the gifts of wisdom and correction of error, but the minister had a different idea. After long droning preliminaries, he sucked in his breath and roared out his impious demand. "*God!*" he bellowed. "Lead *your party* to victory!" Awakened, the delegates cheered until the sunlight from the skylights seemed to dance. Who would have thought that so many believed in God! And how exhilarating to know to which party the King of the Universe belonged! Here I proceed differently than in chapter five, simply resolving each worldly ideology into its constituent moral errors, and contrasting each error with the tradition of the faith.

Chapter eight, *Why We Kill the Weak*, prepares the way for the conclusion by revisiting the themes of *The Revenge of Conscience*, but from another direction. Abortion as liberty, euthanasia as mercy, suicide as medicine: How is it even possible for minds wrought by God to think such thoughts? From Augustine we learn that one can only understand the bad from the good, not the good from the bad; in every case we must try to comprehend the good impulse from whose pollution the bad one comes. What then are the good impulses from whose pollution comes the wish to destroy the weak? Chief are pity, prudence, amenity, honor, remorse, love, and the sense of justice. If they were annihilated we would be merely indifferent; because they are only bent, we kill. I briefly consider how each in turn is diverted from its end.

The concluding chapter is both a reprise and a charge. Christian faith was once widespread among us. Consequently, the people of our generation must hold down not only the present knowledge of general revelation, but also the troubling memory of special revelation. The task of Christians is to find the ways to stir up that troubling memory and arouse that present knowledge—to dissipate smokescreens and break up self-deceptions. We know quite a bit about how to do that in private conversation. Can it be done in the public square, or is that world of sound bites and shouting matches a lost cause?

But introductions must also have their conclusions. A final question for this introduction is why a supposedly Christian reflection on politics is about original sin—but not about redemption. After all, Christianity is a rescue religion, in which the Bad News is only a prolegomenon to the Good News. I know full well from my own release from slavery that nothing in a man is too far sunk to be raised by God, if only he trusts the Redeemer. Nevertheless, where the river of life penetrates the continent of politics, the legend on my map reads *Here Be Dragons.*

One problem is that the nation is not the Church—a problem upon which I have touched already. The City of God may interpenetrate the City of Man, but will never coincide with it. Another is that although the forgiveness of sin takes an instant, the cure of the sin-sickened soul is gradual and not complete until heaven. Complicating the matter is that "decent and respectable" folk are usually least apt to recognize their need for redemption and seek it. Blessed are the poor and broken in spirit! But how confusing for the state, ordained not only to punish wrongdoers but to commend the decent and respectable. Worst of all, the dragons whisper the non sequitur that because even politics can be redeemed, therefore politics itself is redemptive—and this is idolatry. Or they urge redemption for the sake of the state—and this too is idolatry. Once again the ancient maxim is vindicated, that the perversion of the best is the worst.

It is plain to me that I am not a good enough man to delve into such subtle matters. This is not to say I might not have to some day. No Christian man is good enough to do what is committed to him. But it has not been committed to me yet.

2

The Revenge of Conscience

THINGS ARE GETTING WORSE VERY QUICKLY NOW. The list of what we are required to approve is growing ever longer. Consider just the domain of sexual practice. First we were to approve sex before marriage, then without marriage, now against marriage. First with one, then with a series, now with a crowd. First with the other sex, then with the same. First between adults, then between children, then between adults and children. The last item has not been added yet, but will be soon: you can tell from the change in language, just as you can tell the approach of winter from the change in the color of leaves. As any sin passes through its stages from temptation, to toleration, to approval, its name is first euphemized, then avoided, then forgotten. A colleague tells me that some of his fellow scholars call child molestation "intergenerational intimacy": that's euphemism. A good-hearted editor tried to talk me out of using the term "sodomy": that's avoidance. My students don't know the word "fornication" at all: that's forgetfulness.

The pattern is repeated in the house of death. First we were to approve of killing unborn babies, then babies in process of birth; next came newborns with physical defects, now newborns in perfect health. Nobel-prize laureate James Watson proposes that parents of newborns be granted a grace period during which they may have their babies killed, and in 1994 a committee of the American Medical Association proposed harvesting organs from some sick babies even before they die. First we were to approve of suicide, then to approve of assisting it. Now we are to approve of a *requirement* to assist it, for, as Ernest van den Haag has argued, it is "unwarranted" for doctors not to kill patients who seek death. First we were to approve of killing the sick and unconscious, then of killing the conscious and consenting. Now we are to approve of killing the conscious and *protesting*, for in the United States, doctors starved and dehydrated stroke patient Marjorie Nighbert to death despite her pleading "I'm hungry," "I'm thirsty," "Please feed me," and "I want food." Such cases are only to be expected when food and water are now often classified as optional treatments rather than humane care; we have not long to go before joining the Netherlands, where involuntary euthanasia is common. Dutch physician and author Bert Keizer has described his response when a nursing home resident choked on her food: he shot her full of morphine and waited for her to die. Such a deed by a doctor in the land that resisted the Nazis.

Why do things get worse so fast? Of course we have names for the process, like "collapse," "decay," and "slippery slope." By conjuring images—a stricken house, a gangrenous limb, a sliding talus—they make us feel we understand. Now, I am no enemy to word-pictures, but a civilization is not really a house, a limb, or a heap of rocks; it cannot literally fall in, rot, or skid out from underfoot. Images can only illustrate an explanation; they cannot substitute for one. So why *do* things get worse so fast? It would be well to know, in case the process can be arrested.

The usual explanation is that conscience is weakened by neglect. Once a wrong is done, the next wrong comes more easily. On this view conscience is mainly a restraint, a resistance, a passive barrier. It does not so much drive us on as hold us back, and when persistently attacked, the restraining wall gets thinner and thinner and finally disappears. Often this explanation is combined with another: conscience comes from culture; it is built up in us from outside. In this view the heart is malleable. We do not clearly know what is right and wrong, and when our teachers change the lessons, our consciences change their contents. What once we deemed wrong, we deem right; what once we deemed right, we deem wrong.

There is something to these explanations, but neither can account for the sheer dynamism of wickedness—for the fact that we are not gently wafted into the abyss but violently propel ourselves into it. Nor, as I will show, can either one account for the peculiar quality of our present moral confusion.

I suggest a different explanation. Conscience is not a passive barrier but an active force; though it can hold us back, it can also drive us on. Moreover, conscience comes not from without but from within: though culture can trim the fringes, the core cannot be changed. The reason things get worse so fast must somehow lie not in the weakness of conscience but in its strength, not in its shapelessness but in its shape.

THE SHAPE OF CONSCIENCE

Whether paradoxical or not, the view of conscience I defend is nothing new; its roots are ancient. In one of the tragedies of Sophocles, the woman Antigone seeks to give her dead brother a proper burial, but is forbidden by the king because her brother was an enemy of the state. She replies to the tyrant that there is another law higher than the state's, and that she will follow it because of its divine authority. Not even the king may require anyone to violate it. Moreover, it requires not only forbearance from evil but active pursuit of the good: in this case, doing the honors for her brother.

Antigone's claim that this higher law has divine authority can easily be misunderstood, because the Greeks did not have a tradition of verbal revelation. The mythical hero Perseus had never climbed any Mount Sinai; the fabled god Zeus had never announced any Ten Commandments. So, although the law of which Antigone speaks somehow has divine authority, she has not learned it by reading something like a Bible, with moral rules delivered by the gods. Nor is she merely voicing the customs of the tribe—at least not if we are to believe Aristotle, who seems a safer authority on the Greeks than our contemporary skeptics. Instead she seems to be speaking of principles that everyone with a normal mind knows by means of conscience. She seems to be speaking of a law written on the heart—of what philosophers would later call the natural law.

Now by contrast with the pagan Greeks, Jews and Christians do have a tradition of verbal revelation. Moses did climb the mountain; God did announce the commandments. One might think, then, that Jews and Christians would not have a natural law tradition because they would not need it. But just the opposite is true. The idea of a law written on the heart is far stronger and more consistent among Jews, and especially Christians, than it was among the pagans. In fact, the very phrase "law written on the heart" is biblical: it comes from the New Testament book of Romans. Judaism calls the natural law the Noahide Commandments because of a rabbinic legend that God had given certain general rules to all the descendants of Noah—that is, all human beings—long before He made His special covenant with the descendants of Abraham. In similar fashion, Christianity distinguishes between "general revelation," which every human being receives, and "special revelation," which is transmitted by witnesses and recorded only in the Bible. General revelation makes us aware of God's existence and requirements so that we cannot help knowing that we have a problem with sin. Special revelation goes further by telling us how to solve that problem.

The natural law is unconsciously presupposed—even when consciously denied—by modern secular thinkers as well. We can see the presupposition at work whenever we listen in on ethical debate.

Consider, for example, the secular ethic of utilitarianism, which holds that the morally right action is always the one that brings about the greatest possible total happiness. Arguments against utilitarianism by other secularists often proceed by showing that the doctrine yields conclusions contrary to our most deeply held moral intuitions. For instance, it is not hard to imagine circumstances in which murdering an innocent man might make all the others much happier than they were before. Utilitarianism, seeking the greatest possible total happiness, would require us to murder the fellow; nevertheless we do not, because we perceive that murder is plain wrong. So instead of discarding the man, we discard the theory. Here is the point: Such an argument against utilitarianism stakes everything on a *pre-philosophical* intuition about the heinousness of murder. Unless there is a law written on the heart, it is hard to imagine where this intuition comes from.

The best short summary of the traditional, natural law understanding of conscience was given by Thomas Aquinas when he said that the core principles of the moral law are the same for all "both as to rectitude and as to knowledge"—in other words, that they are not only right for all but known to all. Nor is it true, as some suppose, that he was referring only to such formal principles as "good is to be done," for he speaks for the greater part of the tradition when he expressly includes such precepts as "Honor thy father and thy mother," "Thou shalt not kill," and "Thou shalt not steal." These, he says, are matters which "the natural reason of every man, of its own accord and at once, judges to be done or not to be done." To be sure, not every moral principle is part of the core, but all moral principles are at least derived from it, if not by pure deduction (killing is wrong and poison kills, so poisoning is wrong), then with the help of prudence (wrongdoers should be punished, but the appropriate punishment depends on circumstances). Our knowledge of *derived* principles such as "Rise up before the hoary head" may be weakened by neglect and erased by culture, but our knowledge of the core principles is ineffaceable. These are the laws we *can't not know.*

Ranged against this view are two others. One simply denies that the core principles are right for all; the other admits they are right for all, but denies they are known to all. The former, of course, is relativism. I call the latter *mere* moral realism—with emphasis on "mere" because natural law is realistic, too, but more so.

Not much need be said here about relativism. It is not an explanation of our decline, but a symptom of it. The reason it cannot be an explanation is that it finds nothing to explain. To the question "Why do things get worse so fast?", it can only return "They do not get worse, only different."

Mere moral realism is a much more plausible opponent, because by admitting the moral law it acknowledges the problem. Things *are* getting worse quickly—plainly, they say, because there is *not* anything we "can't not know." *Everything* in conscience can be weakened by neglect and erased by culture. Now if mere moral realists are right about this, then although the problem of moral decline may begin in volition, it dwells in cognition: it may begin as a defect of will, but ends as a defect of knowledge. We may have started by neglecting what we knew, but we have now gone so far that we really do not know it any more. What is the result? That our contemporary ignorance of right and wrong is genuine. We *really do not* know the truth, but we are honestly searching for it—trying to see on a foggy night—doing the best that we can. In a sense, we are blameless for our deeds, for we do not know any better.

All this sounds persuasive, yet it is precisely what the older tradition, the natural law tradition, denies. We *do* know better; we are *not* doing the best we can. The problem of moral decline is volitional, not cognitive; it has little to do with knowledge. By and large we do know right from wrong, but wish we did not. We only make believe we are searching for truth—so that we can do wrong, condone wrong, or suppress our remorse for having done wrong in the past.

If the traditional view is true, then our decline is owed not to moral ignorance but to moral suppression. We are not untutored, but "in denial." We do not lack moral knowledge; we hold it down.

MORAL CONFUSION

Offhand it seems as though believing in a law we can't not know would make it harder, not easier, to explain why things are so quickly getting worse. If the moral law really is carved on the heart, wouldn't it be hard to ignore? On the other hand, if it is merely penciled in as the mere moral realists say—well?

But this is merely picture thinking again. Carving and penciling are but metaphors, and more than metaphors are necessary to show why the suppression of conscience is more violent and explosive than its mere weakening would be. First let us consider a few facts that ought to arouse our suspicion, facts about the precise kind of moral confusion we suffer, or say we suffer.

Consider this tissue of contradictions: Most who call abortion wrong call it killing. Most who call it killing say it kills a baby. Most who call it killing a baby decline to prohibit it altogether. Most who decline to prohibit it think it should be restricted. More and more people favor restrictions. Yet greater and greater numbers of people have had or have been involved in abortions.

Or this one: Most adults are worried about teenage sex. Yet rather than telling kids to wait until marriage, most tell kids to wait until they are "older," as we are. Most say that premarital sex between consenting adults is a normal expression of natural desires. Yet hardly any are comfortable telling anyone, especially their own children, how many people they have slept with themselves.

Or this one: Accessories to suicide often write about the act; they produce page after page to show why it is right. Yet a large part of what they write about is guilt. Author George E. Delury, jailed for poisoning and suffocating his wife, says in his written account of the affair that his guilt feelings were so strong they were "almost physical."

As to the first example, if abortion kills a baby then it ought to be banned to everyone; why allow it? But if it does not kill a baby it is hard to see why we should be uneasy about it at all; why restrict it? It is not like driving fast or drinking alcohol, where the problem lies in degree; the issue is killing *as such*. We restrict what we allow because we know it is wrong but do not want to give it up; we feed our hearts scraps in hopes of hushing them, as cooks quiet their kitchen puppies.

As to the second example, sexual promiscuity has exactly the same bad consequences among adults as it has among teenagers. But if it is just an innocent pleasure, then why not talk it up? Swinging is no longer a novelty; the sexual revolution is now gray with age. If shame persists, the only possible explanation is that guilt persists as well.

The third example speaks for itself. Delury calls the very strength of his feelings a proof that they did *not* express "moral" guilt, merely the "dissonance" resulting from violation of an instinctual block inherited from our primate ancestors. We might paraphrase his theory, "the stronger the guilt, the less it matters."

Clearly, whatever our problem may be, it is not that conscience is weak. We may be confused, but we are not confused *that* way. It is not that we do not know the truth, but that we tell ourselves something different.

The Force of Conscience

If the law written on the heart can be repressed, then we cannot count on it to *restrain* us from doing wrong; that much is obvious. I have made the more paradoxical claim that repressing it hurls us into *further* wrong. Holding conscience down does not deprive it of its force; it merely distorts and redirects that force. We are speaking of something less like the erosion of an earthen dike so that it fails to hold the water back, than like the compression of a powerful spring so that it buckles to the side.

Here is how it works. Guilt, guilty knowledge, and guilty feelings are not the same thing; men and women can have the knowledge without the feelings, and they can have the feelings without the fact. Even when suppressed, however, the knowledge of guilt always produces certain objective needs, which make their own demand for satisfaction irrespective of the state of the feelings. These needs include confession, atonement, reconciliation, and justification.

Now when guilt is acknowledged, the guilty deed can be repented so that these four needs can be genuinely satisfied. But when the guilty knowledge is suppressed, they can only be displaced. That is what generates the impulse to further wrong. Taking the four needs one by one, let us see how this happens.

The need to *confess* arises from transgression against what we know, at some level, to be truth. I have already commented on the tendency of accessories to suicide to write about their acts. Besides George Delury, who killed his wife, we may mention Timothy E. Quill, who prescribed lethal pills for his patient, and Andrew Solomon, who participated in the death of his mother. Solomon, for instance, writes in the *New Yorker* that "the act of speaking or writing about your involvement is, inevitably, a plea for absolution." Many readers will remember the full-page signature advertisements feminists took out in the early days of the abortion movement, telling the world that they had killed their own unborn children. Today, perhaps, the equivalent is the tell-all television talk show. At first it seems baffling that the sacrament of confession can be inverted to serve the ends of advocacy. Only by recognizing the power of suppressed conscience can this paradox be understood.

The need to *atone* arises from the knowledge of a debt that must somehow be paid. One would think such knowledge would always lead directly to repentance, but the counselors whom I have interviewed tell a different story. One woman learned during her pregnancy that her husband had been unfaithful to her. He wanted the child, so to punish him for betrayal she had an abortion. The trauma of killing was even greater than the trauma of his treachery, because this time she was to blame. What was her response? She aborted the next child, too; in her words, "I wanted to be able to hate myself more for what I did to the first baby." By trying to atone without repenting, she was driven to repeat the sin.

The need for *reconciliation* arises from the fact that guilt cuts us off from God and man. Without repentance, intimacy must be simulated precisely by sharing with others in the guilty act. Leo Tolstoy knew this. In *Anna Karenina* there comes a time when the lovers' mutual guiltiness is their only remaining bond. But the phenomenon is hardly restricted to cases of marital infidelity. Andrew Solomon says that he, his brothers, and his father are united by the "weird legacy" of their implication in his mother's death, and quotes a nurse who participated in her own mother's death as telling him, "I know some people will have trouble with my saying this but it was the most intimate time I've ever had with anyone." Herbert Hendin comments in a book on the Dutch affair with euthanasia, "The feeling that participation in death permits an intimacy that they are otherwise unable to achieve permeates euthanasia stories and draws patients and doctors to euthanasia." And no wonder. Violation of a basic human bond is so terrible that the burdened conscience must instantly establish an abnormal one to compensate; the very gravity of the transgression invests the new bond with a sense of profound significance. Naturally some will find it attractive.

The need for reconciliation has a public dimension, too. Isolated from the community of moral judgment, transgressors strive to gather a substitute around themselves. They do not sin privately;

they recruit. The more ambitious among them go further. Refusing to go to the mountain, they require the mountain to come to them: society must be transformed so that it no longer stands in awful judgment. So it is that they change the laws, infiltrate the schools, and create intrusive social-welfare bureaucracies.

Finally we come to the need for *justification*, which requires more detailed attention. Unhooked from justice, justification becomes rationalization, which is a more dangerous game than it seems. The problem is that the ordinances written on the heart all hang together. They depend on each other in such a way that we cannot suppress one except by rearranging all the others. A few cases will be sufficient to show how this happens.

Consider sexual promiscuity. The official line is that modern people do not take sex outside marriage seriously any longer; mere moral realists say this is because we no longer realize the wrong of it. I maintain that we do know it is wrong but pretend that we do not. Of course one must be careful to distinguish between the core laws of sex: the ones we can't not know, and the derived ones, which we can not know. For example, though true and reasonable, the superiority of monogamous to polygamous marriage is probably not part of the core. On the other hand, no human society has ever held that the sexual powers may be exercised by anyone with anyone, and the recognized norm is a durable and culturally protected covenant between man and woman with the intention of procreation. Casual shack-ups and one-night stands do not qualify.

Because we can't not know that sex belongs with marriage, when we separate them we cover our guilty knowledge with rationalizations. In any particular culture, particular rationalizations may be just as strongly protected as marriage; the difference is that while the rationalizations vary from culture to culture, the core does not. At least in our culture, such sexual self-deceptions are more common among women than men. I do not think this is because the female conscience is stronger (or weaker) than the male. However, sex outside marriage exposes the woman to greater risk, so whereas the man must fool only his conscience, she must fool both her conscience and her self-interest. If she does insist on doing wrong, she has twice as much reason to rationalize.

One common rationalization is to say "No" while doing "Yes" in order to tell oneself afterward "I didn't go along." William Gairdner reports that according to one rape crisis counselor, many of the women who call her do so not to report that they *have* been raped, but to ask *whether* they were raped. If they have to ask, of course, they probably have not been; they are merely dealing with their ambivalence by throwing the blame for their decisions on their partners. But this is a serious matter. Denial leads to the further wrong of false witness.

Another tactic is inventing private definitions of marriage. Quite a few people "think of themselves as married" although they have no covenant at all. Some even fortify the delusion with "moving-in ceremonies" featuring happy words without promises. Unfortunately, people who "think of themselves as married" refuse the obligations of real marriage, but demand all of its cultural privileges. Rationalization is so much work that they require other people to support them in it. Such demands make the cultural protection of real marriage more difficult.

Yet another ruse is to admit that sex belongs with marriage but to fudge the nature of the connection. By this reasoning I tell myself that sex is okay because I am going to marry my partner, because I want my partner to marry me, or because I have to find out if we could be happy married. An even more dangerous fudge is to divide the form of marriage from its substance—to say "we don't need promises because we're in love." The implication, of course, is that those who do need promises love impurely, that those who do not marry are more truly married than those who do.

This last rationalization is even more difficult to maintain than most. Love, after all, is a permanent and unqualified commitment to the true good of the other person, and the native tongue of commitment is, precisely, promises. To work, therefore, this ruse requires another: having deceived oneself about the nature of marriage, one must now deceive oneself about the nature of love. The usual way of doing so is to mix up love with the romantic feelings that characteristically accompany it, and call *them* "intimacy." If only we have these feelings, we tell ourselves, we may have sex. That is to say, we may have sex—if we feel like it.

Here is where things really become interesting, because if the criterion of being as-good-as-married is sexual feelings, then obviously nobody who has sexual feelings may be prevented from marrying. So homosexuals must also be able to "marry"; their unions, too, should have cultural protection. At this point suppressed conscience strikes another blow, reminding us that marriage is linked with procreation. But now we are in a box. We cannot say "therefore homosexuals cannot marry," because that would strike against the whole teetering structure of rationalizations. Therefore we decree that having been made marriageable, homosexuals must be made procreative; the barren field must seem to bloom. There is, after all, artificial insemination. And there is adoption. So it comes to pass that children are given as a right to those from whom they were once protected as a duty. The normalization of perversion is complete.

MULTIPLYING TRANSGRESSIONS

When ordinary rationalization fails, people revert to other modes of suppression. We often see this when an unmarried young woman becomes pregnant. Suddenly her conscience discovers itself; though she was not ashamed to lift her skirts, she is suddenly ashamed to show her swelling belly. What can she do? Well, she can have an abortion: she can revert to the mode of suppression called "getting rid of the evidence." Once again conscience multiplies transgressions. But she finds that the new transgression is no solution to the

old one; in fact, now she has something even more difficult to rationalize.

Think what is necessary to justify abortion. Because we can't
not know that it is wrong to deliberately kill human beings, there are
only four options. We must deny that the act is deliberate, deny that
it kills, deny that its victims are human, or deny that wrong must not
be done. The last option is literally nonsense. That something must
not be done is what it means for it to be wrong; to deny that wrong
may not be done is merely to say "wrong is not wrong," or "what
must not be done may be done." The first option is hardly promising either. Abortion does not just happen; it must be performed. Its
proponents not only admit there is a "choice," they boast of it. As to
the second option, if it was ever promising, it is no longer. Millions
of women have viewed sonograms of their babies kicking, sucking
their thumbs, and turning somersaults: whatever these little ones
are, they are busily alive. Even most feminists have given up calling
the baby a "blood clot" or describing abortion as the "extraction of
menses."

The only option even barely left is number three: to deny the
humanity of the victims. It is at this point that the machinery slips
out of control. For the only way to make option three work is to
ignore biological nature—which tells us that from conception on-
ward the child is as human as the rest of us (does anyone imagine
that a dog is in there?)—and invent another criterion of humanity,
one that makes it a matter of degree. Some of us must turn out more
human, others less. This is a dicey business even for abortionists. It
hardly needs to be said that no one has been able to come up with a
criterion that makes babies in the womb less human but leaves everyone else as he was; the teeth of the moral gears are too finely set
for that.

Consider, for instance, the criteria of "personhood" and "delib-
erative rationality." According to the former, one is more or less human according to whether he is more or less a person; according to

the latter, he is more or less a person according to whether he is more or less able to act with mature and thoughtful purpose. Unborn babies turn out to be killable because they cannot act maturely; they are less than fully persons, and so less than fully human. In fact, they *must* be killed when the interests of those who are more fully human require it. Therefore, not only may their mothers abort, but it would be wrong to stop the mothers from doing so. But look where else this drives us. Doesn't maturity also fall short among children, teenagers, and many adults? Then aren't they also less than fully persons—and if less than fully persons, then less than fully humans? Clearly so, hence they too must yield to the interests of the more fully human; all that remains is to sort us all out. "No, the progression is too extreme!" someone will protest. "People are not that logical!" Ah, but they are more logical than they know; they are only logical *slowly.* The implication they do not grasp today they may grasp in thirty years; if they do not grasp it even then, their children will. It is happening already. Look around.

So conscience has its revenge. We can't not know the preciousness of human life—therefore, if we tell ourselves that humanity is a matter of degree, we cannot help holding those who are more human more precious than those who are less. The urge to justify abortion drives us inexorably to a system of moral castes more pitiless than anything the East has devised. Of course we can fiddle with the grading criteria: consciousness, self-awareness, and contribution to society have been proposed—racial purity has been tried. No such tinkering avails to change the character of our deeds. If we will a caste system, then we shall have one; if we will that some shall have their way, then in time there shall be a nobility of Those Who Have Their Way. All that our fiddling with the criteria achieves is a rearrangement of the castes.

Need we wonder why, then, having started on our babies, we now want to kill our grandparents? Sin ramifies. It is fertile, fissiparous, and parasitic, always in search of new kingdoms to corrupt. It breeds. But just as a virus cannot reproduce except by commandeering the machinery of a cell, sin cannot reproduce except by taking over the machinery of conscience. Not a gear, not a wheel is destroyed, but they are all set turning in different directions than their wont. Evil must rationalize, and that is its weakness. But it can, and that is its strength.

Natural Consequences

We have seen that although conscience works in everyone, it does not restrain everyone. In all of us some of the time, in some of us all of the time, its fearsome energy merely "multiplies transgressions." Bent backwards by denial, it is more likely to catalyze moral collapse than hold it back.

But conscience is not the only expression of the natural law in human nature. Thomas Aquinas defined law as a form of discipline that compels through fear of punishment. In the case of human law, punishment means suffering the civil consequences of violation; in the case of natural law it means suffering the natural consequences of violation. If I cut myself, I bleed. If I get drunk, I have a hangover. If I sleep with many women, I lose the power to care for anyone, and sow pregnancies, pain, and suspicion.

Unfortunately, the disciplinary effect of natural consequences is diminished in at least two ways. These two diminishers are the main reason why the discipline takes so long, so that the best that can be hoped for in most cultures is a pendulum swing between moral laxity and moral strictness.

The first diminisher is a simple time lag: not every consequence of violating the natural law strikes immediately. Some results make themselves felt only after several generations, and by that time people are so deeply sunk in denial that even more pain is necessary to bring them to their senses. A good example of a long-term consequence is the increase of venereal disease. When I was a boy we all knew about syphilis and gonorrhea, but because of penicillin they were supposed to be on the way out. Today the two horrors are becoming antibiotic-resistant, and herpes, chlamydia, genital warts, human papilloma virus, several kinds of hepatitis, and more than a dozen other sexually transmitted diseases, most of them formerly rare, are ravaging the population. Other long-term consequences of violating the laws of sex are poverty, because single women have no one to help them raise their children; crime, because boys grow into adolescence without a father's influence; and child abuse, because although spouses tend to greet babies with joy, live-ins tend to greet them with jealousy and resentment. Each generation is less able to maintain families than the one before. Truly the iniquities of the fathers—and mothers—are visited upon the children and the children's children to the third and fourth generation.

The second diminisher comes from us: "Dreaming of systems so perfect that no one will need to be good," we exert our ingenuity to *escape* from the natural consequences of breaking the natural law. Not all social practices have this effect. For instance, threatening drunk drivers with legal penalties supplements the discipline of natural consequences rather than undermining it. Nor is the effect always intended. We do not devise social insurance programs in order to encourage improvidence, though they do have this result. It is not even always wrong. It would be abominable to refuse treatment to a lifelong smoker with emphysema, even though he may have been buoyed in his habit by the confidence that the doctors would save him. But to act with the *purpose* of compensating for immorality is always wrong, as when we set up secondary school clinics to dispense pills and condoms to teenagers.

Here is an axiom: We cannot alter human nature, physical, emotional, or spiritual. A corollary is that no matter how cleverly devised, our contrivances never do succeed in canceling out the natural consequences of breaking the natural law. At best they delay them, and for several reasons they can even make them worse. In the first place they alter incentives: people with ready access to pills and condoms see less reason to be abstinent. In the second place they encourage wishful thinking: most people grossly exaggerate their effectiveness in preventing disease and pregnancy and completely ignore the risks. In the third place they reverse the force of example: before long the practice of abstinence erodes even among people who *do not* take precautions. Finally they transform thought: members of the contraceptive culture think liberty from the natural consequences of their decisions is somehow owed to them.

There comes a time when even the law shares their view. In *Planned Parenthood v. Casey,* which reauthorized the private use of lethal violence against life in the womb, the Supreme Court *admitted* that its original abortion ruling might have been wrong, but upheld it anyway. As it explained, "For two decades of economic and social developments, people have organized their intimate relationships and made choices that define their views of themselves and their places in society in reliance on the availability of abortion in the event that contraception should fail.... An entire generation has come of age free to assume [this] concept of liberty." To put the thought more simply, what we did has separated sex from responsibility for resulting life for so long that to change the rules on people now would be unfair.

Our efforts to thwart the law of natural consequences merely make the penalty more crushing when it comes. The only question is whether our culture will be able to survive the return stroke of the piston. To survive what is bearing down on us, we must learn four hard lessons: to acknowledge the natural law as a true and universal morality; to be on guard against our own attempts to overwrite it with new laws that are really rationalizations for wrong; to fear the natural consequences of its violation, recognizing their inexorability; and to forbear from all further attempts to compensate for immorality, returning on the path that brought us to this place.

Unfortunately, the condition of human beings since before recorded history is that we do not want to learn hard lessons. We would rather remain in denial. What power can break through such a barrier?

The only Power that ever has. Thomas Aquinas writes that when a nation suffers tyranny, those who enthroned the tyrant may first try to remove him, then call upon the emperor for help. When these human means fail, they should consider their sins and pray. We are now so thoroughly under the tyranny of our vices that it would be difficult for us to recognize an external tyrant at all. By our own hands we enthroned them: our strength no longer suffices for their removal; they have suspended the senate of right reason and the assembly of the virtues; the emperor, our will, is held hostage; and it is time to pray. We do not want to read the letters on the heart, because they burn; but they do burn, so at last we must read them.

3

The Illusion of Moral Neutrality

NIETZSCHE CLAIMED that if men took God seriously, they would still be burning heretics at the stake. In the same spirit, one supposes, are the notions that if men really cherished moral truth, they would suppress all beliefs they considered wrong, and that if men still cared about the sanctity of the marriage bed, they would go back to making adulterers wear the scarlet A.

Today two different groups of people agree with conditional statements of this sort. In the first group are the ordinary bigots, who are always among us. The second are a kind of modern backlash—call it the reaction—found principally among the "cultural elite." For instance, whereas the bigots respond to Nietzsche's conditional by saying, "Yes, that's why we should burn heretics," the reactionaries respond to it by saying, "No, that's why we should suppress the public expression of belief in God."

These reactionaries claim to love tolerance, but, misunderstanding it, they strangle it in their embrace. Their creed is that intolerance is born at the same moment as public moral commitments, that morality must therefore be a "private" affair, and that in order to say that tolerance is a good, we must forbear to say aloud that anything else is good or evil. Their god is Neutrality. In certain intellectual regions he travels under other names such as Autonomy and Rights.

We meet this jealous and negating god on the philosophic right, where conservatives like Michael Oakeshott tell us that the specific and limited activity of "governing" has "nothing to do" with natural law or morals. We encounter him on the philosophic left, where liberals like John Rawls and Marxists like Jürgen Habermas invent devices like the Veil of Ignorance and the Ideal Speech Situation to convince us that if we wish to understand truly the principles of justice, we must pretend to forget not only who we are, but also everything we ever thought we knew about good and evil. We meet this god in law, where many jurists treat ethical distinctions such as "family" vs. "non-family" as "invidious classifications" that deny citizens the equal protection of the law. We meet him in education, where elementary school children are offered books like *Daddy's Roommate, Heather Has Two Mommies,* and *Gloria Goes to Gay Pride.* In fact, we meet this god everywhere: in the university, in the movie theatre, in many churches and synagogues, and, it goes without saying, on the even more ubiquitous altar of the television.

It might seem remarkable that people who insist that tolerance means moral neutrality should themselves be so earnest in ridiculing those who are not neutral. But of course, they themselves are not neutral either. The scandal of Neutrality is that its worshipers cannot answer the question "Why be neutral?" without committing themselves to particular goods—social peace, self-expression, self-esteem, ethnic pride, or what have you—thereby violating their own desideratum of Neutrality. Yet even this is merely a symptom of a deeper problem, that there is no such thing as Neutrality. It is not merely unachievable, like a perfect circle; it is inconceivable, like a square circle. Whether we deem it better to take a stand or be silent, we have offended this god in the very act of deeming.

To see the folly of neutralism is one thing; to escape from it is another. Many who understand perfectly well that tolerance cannot be defended by suspending judgment about goods and evils have difficulty defending it in any other way. They suspect the worst: that if neutrality is a square circle, then so is tolerance, along with all of its component virtues like objectivity and fairness. They fear that by leaving the reactionaries, they will join with the ordinary bigots. They are right to fear this trap, but make the difficulty of avoiding it greater than it is.

UNDERSTANDING TOLERANCE

Properly understood, what is this thing called tolerance? What does it really demand of us? What do we need in order to come by it? Let us see if we can work this out.

The truth is, we already know the answer in part. To tolerate something is to put up with it even though we might be tempted to suppress it. The next step, then: which things are we tempted to suppress? Here, too, we know the answer: we are tempted to suppress those things that we deem mistaken, painful, wrong, harmful, offensive, or in some other way unworthy of approval.

Now, we use the term "temptation" when our hearts solicit us either to do something we ought to forbear or to forbear from something we ought to do. But *shouldn't* we suppress the things that we deem mistaken, painful, wrong, harmful, offensive, and so on? The answer is, sometimes we should, and sometimes we should not. For instance, it is certainly not acceptable to tolerate the act of rape. But it is certainly right to put up with the profession, by rational argument, of opinions that we deem mistaken.

What makes these two cases different? In one respect, of course, they are just the same. Whichever we endeavored to suppress— rape, or the profession of false opinions—we would presumably be trying to avert particular evils, or, if you prefer, to protect particular goods. The goods that are injured in the act of rape include the dignity of the woman, her physical and emotional well-being, and the integrity of a certain pattern of relationships between men and women, a pattern that depends on trust rather than fear. Similarly the goods that are injured in the act of professing false opinions include the clear knowledge of the truth, the public recognition of its value, and the integrity of a certain pattern of conduct, a pattern that depends on right judgment rather than error. By suppressing rape we would be trying to protect the first set of goods; by suppressing the profession of false opinions, the latter.

And so it is with every case. People may not *agree* about what is good and what is evil; they may be *mistaken* about what is good and what is evil; they may even call evil good, and good evil. But every time someone wants to suppress something, we can be sure he is attempting to prevent what he thinks, rightly or wrongly, to be evil, or alternatively, to protect something he thinks, rightly or wrongly, to be good. Why, then—to return to the question—do we sometimes tolerate an evil, or put up with an injury to a good?

The answer is not, as some people hold, skepticism. Take the case of conducting a debate, a practice notorious for tolerating the evil of false opinions. There are three kinds of skeptics: the utter skeptic, who is in doubt about all things; the partial skeptic, who is in doubt about some things; and the non-skeptic, who is in doubt about nothing whatsoever. Can the utter skeptic say, "Because all is in doubt, all should be heard"? No, he must rather say, "The rightness of hearing and the rightness of silencing are equally in doubt; I cannot tell you which to choose." Can the partial skeptic say, "I do not believe in debate"? Yes, but he might instead say, "I am in doubt about what is true in general. But I am sure that truth is good, I am sure that exchange of discursive reasoning will help to find it, and I am sure about the kind of manners that such exchange requires." And can the non-skeptic say "To put up with falsehood is wrong"? Yes, but he might instead say this: "Although I am sure of every truth, one such truth is that the exercise of rebutting error will sharpen the insight I already possess, and another is that it may convert my opponent." We see that only the non-skeptic and the partial skeptic can deal with debate. Neither does it because of what he doubts; each does it because of what he does not doubt. Each tolerates falsehood for the sake of truth.

Once we see this, the real reason that we sometimes tolerate evils or put up with injuries to good becomes clear: we do it to prevent graver evils, or to advance greater goods. For there is a certain paradox in this business of suppressing evils: *The act of suppression itself* may be evil or may give rise to evils. In fact, it often does. Because this is so, we must always put the two evils, the evil that suppression engenders and the evil that it prevents, on a scale. When the evil that suppression engenders equals or exceeds the evil that it prevents—or when the actions that suppression would require are themselves forbidden by moral law—then we ought to put up with the thing in question instead of suppressing it. Of course I do not suppose that all goods and evils are commensurable, that the good of an action lies only in its results, or that we may "do evil that good may result." One may consider consequences without considering them in the way that "consequentialists" do.

The paradox before us is the very basis of the virtue of tolerance. But on closer examination we see that there are two cases, in one of which the paradox is more pronounced than the other.

The less paradoxical case is one in which the goods that are protected by suppression and those injured by suppression are different. For example, at the same time that we consider suppressing the profession of false opinions for the sake of truth, we might consider tolerating their profession for the sake of peace. Truth and peace are both goods, but of course they are not the same good. First we have to decide which of the two goods is of higher order, because that one trumps the other. If they are of the same order, then we must resort to judgments of degree. One need not suppose that judgment has mathematical precision, only that there is such a thing as judgment.

In the other, more paradoxical, case, the goods that are protected by suppression and the goods that are injured by suppression are the same. For example, at the same time that we consider suppressing the profession of false opinions for the sake of truth, we might consider tolerating their profession—at least their profession by rational argument—also for the sake of truth. On the side of suppression we might plead, "After all, the opinions in question *are false,* aren't they? Then isn't it a gain to get rid of them?" But on the side of toleration, we might ask, "But what better engine have we for *honing* truth than to try it against error in a fair fight?" In this case we do not have to decide which of two goods is of higher order, because there is only one good at issue. But we do have to compare different hypotheses about what really promotes that good.

Each of these cases reveals a different element in the practice of tolerance: the first, in which the good that suppression protects is different from the one it injures, holds up *right judgment in the protection of greater ends against lesser ends;* the second, in which the goods protected by suppression and injured by suppression are the same, holds up *right judgment in the protection of ends against mistaken means.* Element two goes more to the heart of the matter. The ends with which a given end comes into conflict—these are largely a matter of circumstance. The means by which a given end cannot, by its nature, be pursued—these are constant.

If the constant element in the practice of tolerance is right judgment in the protection of ends against mistaken means, then the constant element in intolerance is *false* judgment in the protection of ends against mistaken means. Right away we see that intolerance shows itself in two different ways, for we can err in either of two different directions. One way is by an excess of indulgence—putting up with something we should suppress. Let us call this the error of *softheadedness.* The other way that we can err is by a deficiency of indulgence—suppressing what we should put up with. Let us call this the error of *narrowmindedness.* Each of these two opposite errors is a deviation from true tolerance; each of them therefore has the same claim to the name of "intolerance."

This may at first sound odd, because our language has so far reserved the word "intolerance" for narrowmindedness. By contrast, consider courage, which is easier to talk about than tolerance. Although we do sometimes forget that rashness as well as cowardice is opposed to true courage, at least we are not burdened by a term, say "in-courage," that could be applied only to cowardice and not to rashness. It seems that either we *prefer* the error of softheadedness to the error of narrowmindedness, or else we do not realize that softheadedness is an error at all. But this is a deep confusion. It is just as much a deviation from true tolerance to put up with rape as it is to suppress the profession of false opinions advanced by rational argument.

Thus far we have three possibilities: two kinds of wrong judgment in the protection of ends against mistaken means, and one kind of right judgment in the protection of ends against mistaken means. Expressed in this way, what we have are three points that appear to be floating in space. Of course there is a flaw in this mental diagram. The three need to be arranged along a *range* which is bounded by two extremes, the one excessive, the one deficient; the one softheaded, the other narrowminded. The reason is that just how indulgent we are toward something—just how much we put up with it, just where we fall between the two extremes—is a matter of degree. For instance, we might make some act a crime. Or we might shun those who do it, but without going so far as criminalization. Or we might try to persuade the wrongdoers to change their ways without going so far as to shun them. Or we might ignore them. Or we might encourage them. We might even reward them. The truly tolerant point will always be somewhere between the two endpoints of the continuum, its location depending on the act in question and on the circumstances. But precisely where it is along this line will vary. The location of true tolerance can be determined only by the exercise of *case-by-case judgment* about the goods and the evils involved. Just as true courage is a mean between rashness and cravenness, and true friendliness is a mean between obsequiousness and boorishness, so true tolerance is a mean between softheadedness and narrow-mindedness. This leads us to the following propositions:

1. Tolerance cannot be neutral about what is good, for its very purpose is to guard goods and avert evils.

2. Tolerance is not a moral rule, a moral attitude, a moral feeling, or a moral capacity, but a moral virtue. Further, although tolerance is not one of the moral virtues that Aristotle discussed, it is a moral virtue of the Aristotelian type. For it is a mean between two opposed vices, one of them characterized by excess and the other by deficiency, its location to be discovered in the case-by-case exercise of practical wisdom.

3. The circumstantial element in the practice of tolerance is right judgment in the protection of greater ends against lesser ends. This is no different from any exercise of practical wisdom, except insofar as its constant element, right judgment in the protection of ends against mistaken means, makes it special.

To be sure, this is only a formal answer to the question of what tolerance is. It directs us toward the exercise of practical wisdom—of well-founded judgment about the goods and evils involved in putting up with things. To give a substantive answer to the question of what tolerance is, however, would be no small matter; even if one had the necessary wisdom to do it, the space of a single chapter could never suffice.

Still, the merely formal definition of tolerance does do certain work for us. First, the fact that tolerance is a moral virtue of the Aristotelian type tells us a great deal about its relation to the others. For those of us who wonder how, if at all, tolerance might be taught, this relation carries powerful implications. Second, for the reason suggested earlier, religion presents the acid test for tolerance. For the loyalty that it concerns is ultimate; if tolerance cannot survive it, then tolerance cannot survive. However, the special role of tolerance in protecting ends against mistaken means gives us the one clue we need to unscrew this inscrutable.

Explaining the first of these two points is the burden of the next section. Explaining the second is the burden of the last.

TEACHING TOLERANCE

All moral virtues—or at the very least, all those of the Aristotelian type—are interdependent. The classical demonstration of this truth, which derives from Thomas Aquinas, pivots on the relation of these virtues to practical wisdom. For every moral virtue depends on practical wisdom; hence if practical wisdom is impaired, then every moral virtue is impaired. But on the other side, practical wisdom depends on every moral virtue; hence if any moral virtue is impaired, practical wisdom is impaired. It follows, then, that through practical wisdom, a flaw in any moral virtue entails a flaw in every other.

How does every moral virtue depend on courage? Think of the virtue of courage. Courage involves a mean between cowardice and recklessness—as we said before, enough fear to avoid being rash, enough daring to avoid being craven. But because the right balance between fear and daring varies from case to case, the habit of courage must be informed by practical wisdom. Now turn the example around. How does practical wisdom depend on every moral virtue? Again, consider courage. In thinking of its exercises, our imaginations usually go no further than pain and death. Aristotle thought no evil could be greater. But this is false: to be held in contempt is more fearful than death, and vice, if it is not more fearful than death, certainly ought to be. To achieve practical wisdom, one needs enough fear to be vigilant of error and enough daring to risk it in pursuit of truth; to hold onto such wisdom, one needs enough fear to dread its loss and enough daring to risk contempt in its defense.

The same two-way relation exists between practical wisdom and moral virtues other than courage. Using a bicycle wheel as our model, the moral virtues are to spokes as practical wisdom is to the hub. We all know what happens when we use a bicycle wheel with a damaged spoke. Before long, the others give in too, and the wheel gets more and more out of true. This is the classical thesis of the *unity of the virtues*. If one virtue bends, then every virtue bends.

Everyday experience corroborates this. We do not even have to go through the hub, for without implying their equality we may say that all the moral virtues are connected at the rim. Tolerance is addled in the unfriendly man; friendship is addled in the dishonest man; honesty is addled in the unjust man; justice is addled in the loveless man; love is addled in the hopeless man; hope is addled in the impatient man; and patience is addled in the intolerant man. So the wheel is closed.

Thus tolerance is one of the moral virtues and depends on all the rest of them. This has implications for the cultivation of tolerant citizens. How so? The unity of the virtues works in only one direction. That is, while impairment of one moral virtue entails impairment of all the rest, *progress* toward one moral virtue does *not* in and of itself entail progress toward all the rest. Think of the bicycle wheel again. Beginning with a perfect round, bending one spoke will soon bend all the others too, but *straightening* one spoke of a crushed wheel will *not* simply pull the others back in true. In fact it may cause some spokes to bend even more. With damaged bicycle wheels, there are three alternatives. We can replace the wheel; we can take it apart, straighten each part separately, and put it back together; or we can leave it in one piece and straighten every part at once. With a soul, the first two alternatives are out of the question because we can neither replace it nor take it apart. The only alternative is to leave it in one piece and straighten every part at once.

Here is what follows: If all the virtues depend on one another, then tolerance cannot be taught unless all the rest are taught as well.

We cannot compensate for the collapse of all our virtues by teaching tolerance and letting the rest go by, as some educators and social critics seem to think: The only cure for moral collapse is moral renewal, on all fronts simultaneously.

That is a hard adage. For even with crushed wheels, the simultaneous straightening of every spoke is hardly thinkable. With crushed souls—which is what we all are—we have no idea how our own efforts might bring it to pass. More than education, we need redemption. For virtues are complicated things: complex dispositions of character, deeply ingrained "habits," by which one calls upon all of his passions and capacities of mind in just those ways that aid, prompt, focus, inform, and execute his moral choices instead of clouding them, misleading them, or obstructing their execution. This means that virtues cannot be imparted just by encouraging certain feelings or developing certain capacities: feelings and capacities are instruments of the virtues, not their realization.

What adds to the difficulty is that virtues are much more than readiness to follow the rules. There are, of course, some rules that are true in all circumstances. Murder is always wrong. But virtues are more like a fitness to distinguish true rules from false, and to choose rightly even where there are no rules or where the rules are no more than rules of thumb and seem to contradict each other. To be sure, if rules are applied judiciously, they can help to restrain the most obvious evils. And this in turn is bound to help in the nurture of virtue. But it does not follow that virtue can be taught simply by means of an exhaustive list of rules. Not only would such a list be endless, but the vicious would rebel before we even reached the second page.

In sum, we are not going to transmit the virtue of tolerance through a quick fix, like a Freshman Orientation Weekend; through a long fix, like a three-volume set of workplace sensitivity regulations; or through a false fix, like a Children of the Rainbow Curriculum. If Plato was right that justice is medicine for the soul, then such instrumentalities are its patent medicine: 5 percent poison, 10 percent flavoring, 85 percent intoxicating spirits, and pure delusion from the first to the last.

RELIGIOUS TOLERATION

Time now to turn to the question of religious tolerance, where even the rules are far from easy to discern.

What *is* religion anyway? Some people say that all religions depend on faith, while all secularisms depend on reason. But as Chesterton remarked in *Orthodoxy*, "It is idle to talk always of the alternative of reason and faith. Reason is itself a matter of faith. It is an act of faith to assert that our thoughts have any relation to reality at all." Other people say that all religions believe in God, while all secularisms do not. But though Theravada Buddhists do not believe in any God, yet we call Buddhism a religion.

Still others, like Tillich and Niebuhr, hold the mark of religion to be the practice of *ultimate concern* that orders all other concerns, *unconditioned loyalty* that trumps all other loyalties. Here we finally hit the mark. For Christians, the ultimate concern is the saving God of Abraham, Isaac, and Jacob who has revealed Himself in the Messiah. Though Buddhists do not believe in the God of Abraham, Isaac, and Jacob, much less in the Messiah, they do have an ultimate concern—escape from suffering, inherent in desire, which, they hold, springs in turn from the illusion of existence.

But if religion is the practice of ultimate concern, then we have another problem. In the first place, even a secularism may be the practice of an ultimate concern. We acknowledge this, for instance, by calling Leninism a religion; similarly we say of a greedy man that "his god is money" and call misplaced devotion "idolatry." In the second place, even among those secularisms that do *not* go so far as to identify ultimate concerns, none is without implications as to what *could or could not* count as an ultimate concern. John Stuart Mill could never decide which, if any, of the "permanent interests of man as a progressive being" was deserving of unconditioned loyalty—but he was sure that the Messiah was not among them.

What all this tells us is that "religious" and "secular" constitute a false dichotomy. We would do better with a trichotomy. An *acknowledged* religion like Christianity or Buddhism posits an ultimate concern and admits it. An *unacknowledged* religion like Leninism posits an ultimate concern but denies that so doing is religious. And an *incomplete* religion like Millianism has not finished ranking its concerns. Incomplete religion can live only in the dreamworld of thought. In the light of day it must become complete or die. For in every life or way of life—whether lived simply, lived with the guidance of an ethical theory, or even lived in defiance of an ethical theory—given enough time, some concern eventually emerges as paramount. Eventually there is something to which every knee bows. This is the person's god. As a matter of theory, one may deny that any concern deserves ultimacy. But as a matter of practice, no one escapes ceding ultimacy to something, whether it deserves ultimacy or not. Choices between incompatible urgencies are unavoidable. To prevent the rise of one or another of these urgencies to supremacy, a person would have to practice a truly Stoic discipline of contradiction—and in the end we would have to ask what urgency he served in so disordering himself. In short, one need not be conscious of his god, or even conscious that he has a god. One might think he has no god, or that he is "looking for" or "waiting for" a god. One may even be converted from one god to another. But one will have a god—or at least be on the road to having one.

With all of this ultimate concern floating about, how can there be religious tolerance at all? The answer is, there *cannot* be—unless one's ultimate concern commands it, or at least allows it. For in this case and this case alone, tolerance toward other claimants to ultimacy is obedience to one's own.

Thus St. Hilary of Poitiers: "God does not want unwilling worship, nor does He require a forced repentance." The idea is that although God demands and deserves our unconditioned loyalty, He is of such a nature that nothing exacted by threats could truly serve Him. For He desires sons and daughters, not slaves: His love is inexorable and consumes everything contrary to itself. This is not the Kantian idea that choice is lovable, but rather the Christian idea that love is chosen. I do not say that His supposed followers have always practiced the loving tolerance He demands. I do say that intolerance stands under His judgment.

But notice: the same consuming fire that for its own sake demands tolerance, for its own sake sets the limits to what is tolerated. If Hilary was right that God does not want unwilling worship, then Hilary's tolerance must be absolute with respect to permitting *belief* in other gods, but this does not mean permitting every act of service to these gods. Hilary must claim the right to say that there are evil services which nothing deserving of unconditioned loyalty could demand, and the correlative right to try to stop anyone who attempts them. For instance, whatever claims of conscience Hilary may honor, he cannot permit a person to plead them in justification of murder. "God told me to kill anyone who got in my way" cuts no ice with him; nor is the case different when other ultimate concerns, other gods, are pleaded in place of God. The Defense of the Revolution, the Greater Good of the Whole, the Purity of the Race, the Hunger of Molech, the Right to Control One's Body—neither these nor any other claimants to ultimacy are accepted as justifying the sacrifice of innocents. "Even conceding your God-given right to be left alone by me in your honor to another supposed god," I imagine Hilary saying, "that right concerns your own soul only. I will not permit you, in its service, to inflict injuries which the true God abhors and forbids."

My example is Christian because I am a Christian. But the logic works just the same if you posit some other ultimate concern, some god other than the true one. For instance, the god of the Benthamite utilitarian is "aggregate pleasure." Hence if the Benthamite could tolerate other creeds at all, his tolerance would be both ordained and limited by the requirements of such pleasure. Likewise, religious tolerance for the Millian utilitarian would be both ordained and limited by the nature of man's "permanent interests" as a "progressive being," and religious tolerance for the Leninist would be both ordained and limited by the needs of "proletarian dictatorship."

One might suppose that this logic works only for so-called teleological creeds, said to give priority to achieving the good over doing the right. This is not so. No recent writer has more sternly insisted on the priority of right over good than John Rawls. Yet even he has an ultimate concern. His concern is "autonomy," the conditions for the realization of which are supposedly determined by choices made behind a Veil of Ignorance that obliterates personal memory. But the conclusion is obvious: for the Rawlsian, religious tolerance is both ordained and limited by what people could want who no longer remembered the love of God. The logic is unchanged; it is only the premise that is perverse.

Where does all this leave us? The bottom line is that Neutrality is no more coherent in the matter of religious tolerance than it is in tolerance of any other sort. What you can tolerate pivots on your ultimate concern. Because different ultimate concerns ordain different zones of tolerance, social consensus is possible only at the points where these zones overlap. Note well: The greater the resemblance of contending concerns, the greater the overlap of their zones of tolerance. The less the resemblance of contending concerns, the less the overlap of their zones of tolerance. Should contending concerns become sufficiently unlike, their zones of tolerance no longer intersect at all. Consensus vanishes.

This, I believe, is our current trajectory. The embattled term "culture war" is not inflammatory; it is merely exact. And we can expect the war to grow worse. The reason for this is that our various gods ordain not only different zones of tolerance, but different norms to regulate the dispute among themselves. True tolerance is not well tolerated. For although the God of some of the disputants ordains that they love and persuade their opponents, the idols of some of the others ordain no such thing.

4

Politics of Virtues, Government of Knaves

T HE FIRST LADY AT THE TIME OF WRITING has been described in the *New York Times Magazine* as a proponent of
the "politics of virtue." Compassion is the virtue to which
the *Times* author refers, and while in ordinary life it means that A
gives of his own to help B, in Mrs. Clinton's style of activism it means
that A takes from C to make B dependent. Apparently, what the
"politics of virtue" means to the author is a high-tax welfare state.

Political theory uses an almost identical expression, the "politics
of virtues," for something quite different: an approach to statecraft
that gives first place to considerations of excellence of character. To
be sure, the proponent *cares* about the other things, but he begins by
thinking of the virtues. Before all else, he wants to know how wise,
how just, how temperate, and how courageous the citizens are, and
whether they are becoming better people or worse. The principal
reason is simple. As de Maistre put it, every country gets the government it deserves: one cannot expect liberty, justice, or concern for
the common good where knaves rule a rabble. So much we should
have learned by now.

Yet we are a broken race in a fallen world. For denying The

Atonement a man may be faithless, but for denying its need he is insane. We are all caught in the wreck. Hence the single greatest problem of politics is simply this: How can we make government promote the common good when there is so little virtue to be found?

By my count, Western thought records just seven general solutions. First is *deterrence*, according to which acts of vice are inhibited by the threat of legal punishment. Second is *filtration*, which counsels that officeholders are recruited disproportionately from among the most virtuous. Then there is *compensation*, whereby citizens are organized in such a way that excess and deficiency correct each other, and all the scattered chips of insight come together in a whole. Next comes *balance*: selfish groups are set against each other so that vice is checked and virtue given leverage. Fifth is *channeling*, in accordance with which non-virtuous motives are shaped and directed so that they give rise to the same behavior as virtue would require. Next, *inculcation*: through law in the broadest sense, government tries to teach virtue directly. Finally, *subsidiarity*: government honors virtue and protects its teachers, but without attempting to take their place.

By reason of our many follies, we may at last have reached that point in history where these solutions can be judged.

DETERRENCE

Consider *deterrence,* the inhibition of acts of vice by the threat of legal punishment. Even this simplest and most straightforward of the seven solutions is sometimes misunderstood, so let us begin by making sure just what it does and does not propose. In the first place, its target is not vice proper, but only the acts of vice. For the very good reason that vice is an invisible disposition of the heart that cannot be detected by the authorities, we do not punish folly, injustice, or intemperance as such, but rather, say, the foolish act of selling liquor to a six-year-old, the unjust act of taking a bribe, and the intemperate act of having a drunken orgy in a public place. Second, because the purpose of law is the *common* rather than the personal good, not even every act of vice is a fitting concern of law; to make it so there must be significant injury to the rest of the public. In practice this is less a limit than it seems, for once we consider indirect harms, like the harm of bad example or the harm of reducing one's ability to fulfill one's duties, we realize that there may be no such thing as an act of vice that does *no* public injury. Nevertheless it is a limit, for not all injury is serious injury.

How effective is this solution? Not very. In the first place, deterrence, supposedly our answer to depravity, is crippled by depravity itself; it works well only when the effects of depravity are incomplete. For as lawbreakers in and out of government know full well, only a fraction of crimes are punished. True, the fraction may be enlarged by such means as putting more policemen on the streets and more auditors in the Department of the Treasury. Beyond a certain point, however, the cost of enlarging it becomes too high— and the more reprobate the population, the sooner this point is reached. Thus law achieves most of its deterrent effect not by exploiting fear, but by exploiting guilt. It presupposes not the total absence of moral qualities among the citizens, but only their imperfection. It shores up a faltering conscience, but it presupposes conscience. Further, punishments must be in keeping with the stage of development that conscience has already reached. To be sure, Thomas Aquinas held that punishments can instruct the conscience as well as employ it—a thesis we will consider later. But even he conceded that punishments can neither instruct *nor* deter if they get too far ahead of the point that conscience has already reached. As the debacle of Prohibition confirms, the attempt to suppress those acts of vice which the citizens still love and find blameless merely makes them "break out into yet greater evils."

Not only must law achieve most of its deterrent effect not by exploiting fear but by exploiting the residue of virtue, worse yet, the guardians themselves must have an even purer heart than those they guard. This is a hard demand, even harder in the marble corridors than on the streets. It is one thing asking policemen not to murder or take bribes, quite another asking lawmakers to abstain from partiality. As Hume observed, men act less virtuously in their public capacities than in their private. Several explanations can be offered for this. One is that few virtuous men have the stomach to campaign; another, that great temptations bring out hidden faults; still another, that personal responsibility is easier to evade when individuals act in concert. Hume's own explanation is more subtle. What steers most men toward the common good, he says, is merely the desire for honor, which is not a craving for goodness as such but for the good opinion of others. Unfortunately, whereas in private life a man may crave the good opinion of everyone, in politics he craves it only of his confederates; hence the common good becomes, for him, the good that is common to party. True, some few do keep their hearts pure even in the sewer of faction. But because the policy of a group is determined by its majority, these few count for nothing. Groups are not kind to exceptions.

We see then that deterrence is not a true solution to the problem of the scarcity of virtue, for the scarcer the virtue, the weaker the deterrent. At best, deterrence is a kind of Hamburger Helper. It helps government go a little further toward the common good with what little virtue we have; it cannot enable government to do without virtue.

FILTRATION

Now we come to *filtration,* the practice of recruiting officeholders disproportionately from among the most virtuous. In this solution to the problem, no pretense is made that we can do without virtue; filtration is an open strategy for getting more from the little bit there is. If power waters all the seeds of vice, all the more important that those in power are not too seedy at the outset. Political history knows of four filtration strategies.

There is *ascription*, that candidates must have particular characteristics which are supposedly correlated with merit but cannot be attained by any voluntary action. The ascriptive characteristic of lineage was the basis on which Aristotle distinguished virtuous aristocracy from its perversion, oligarchy. Both, of course, made rule the affair of an elite, but whereas in aristocracy the few are set apart by noble breeding, in oligarchy they are merely filthy rich. Several ascriptive filters are also specified by the Constitution; for instance, the President must be a natural-born citizen, and Senators must be at least thirty years of age.

Another strategy is that of *achievement*. Not only did every senator in Republican Rome come from a magisterial lineage—by itself, an ascriptive requirement—but each had also personally ascended the *cursus honorum*, holding in turn every one of the prescribed magisterial offices from lowest to highest. Although the analogy is perhaps not to be pressed too strongly, some Americans view the system of presidential primaries in a similar light: not, to be sure, as a ladder of honors, but as a gamut of obstacles.

Then there is filtration by *examination*, in which candidates must perform well on a formal test of knowledge or belief, as mandarin bureaucrats demonstrated erudition in the works of the sages. Although the Constitution forbids using religion as an filter, we do require a civil service exam. While the mandarin exam may have been viewed as the best filter possible, the American exam is viewed merely as an improvement upon patronage.

Finally, there is *approbation*, in which candidates must demonstrate their merit to those deemed qualified to judge it. Madison expected citizens to vote according to their estimates of the candidates' virtue. The key assumption here is as old as Plato's *Laws*: that when undistracted by bribes, ordinary people are both able to identify and willing to defer to persons of greater virtue than themselves.

Of course, Madison does not assume that *every* kind of merit can be judged by inexperienced people. For the kinds that cannot, he simply adds more layers to the filter.

Are we better off with a filter than without? Sometimes, but not always. Consider some of the ways in which filters can backfire.

The whole point of a filter is, of course, to magnify some difference between ruled and rulers. But any difference between the ranks may whet the tooth of envy. This is especially true with a difference in virtue—whether it is real or only sham. A virtue filter that awakens envy is like a winnowing basket that separates the chaff by destroying the grain.

Ambition gives rise to another possible backfire. The wise, said Plato, must be forced to rule. What does this say about those who want to? Walter Mondale has said that to run the gauntlet of presidential primaries, one must have "fire in the belly." Does he mean persistence, endurance, and adaptability? Or does he mean the love of power and the lust of domination?

Then there are wise fools. Examination filters presuppose that wisdom is correlated with learning. True, moral discernment without any propositional knowledge at all is clearly impossible. In modern, relativistic education, on the other hand, the more someone learns the less discerning he becomes.

And there is the race of technique. Every advance in the technique of filtration calls forth an advance in the technique of evasion. Consider the electoral filter. *Leak*: voters can be bribed. *Patch*: make electoral districts large. As Madison suggested, the greater the number of voters who have to be bought all at once, the more expensive it is "for unworthy candidates to practice with success the vicious arts by which elections are too often carried." *New leak*: unable to finance these vicious arts themselves, candidates seek the assistance of large-scale political organizations—or promise to pay the promised bribes *after* the election, when they will have control of the public treasury.

Last, there is the vesting of interests. The steps we have taken to keep patronage out of government hiring make it hard to control bureaucrats, and the steps we have taken to keep it out of firing make it hard to dismiss them for incompetence. Indeed, a permanent, nonpartisan civil service, protected by law and largely unionized, naturally reinterprets the virtues of professionalism in terms of survival, growth, and expansion of mission.

Filtration's inherent problems help us to understand the pendulum quality of some of our reforms. Consider the Progressive Era replacement of partisan caucuses by partisan primaries. This merely reflects a preference for the approbation of followers over the approbation of bosses. In view of the swelling lunacy of electronic politics, the old smoke-filled room is looking better and better.

COMPENSATION

Compensation organizes citizens in such a way that excess and deficiency correct each other, and all the scattered chips of insight come together in a whole. The idea is that wherever there are differences, there must be coordination. To be sure, not all difference in temperament is due to vice, nor all difference in insight to folly. But each sort of difference requires its own sort of coordination. Francis and Benedict must be coordinated because they develop virtue in different ways; Laurel and Hardy, because they bungle it in different ways. Whereas gifts must be arranged to unfold each other, flaws must be arranged to offset each other.

Suppose we were to follow Aristotle and St. Thomas in distinguishing between rectitude of judgment and rectitude of passion (leaving rectitude of will for later). Each kind of rectitude is lost in a different way: rectitude of judgment by seeing only part of the picture, rectitude of passion through excess or deficiency, as in rashness and cowardice. For each kind of deviation from rectitude there is also a different method of compensation.

The compensation for defects of judgment is *composing insights*. At a certain point in Aristotle's *Politics*, he sets the Many and the Few in an imaginary conversation about who has the best claim to rule. The aristocrats claim rule on grounds of superior wisdom, for they have both experience and erudition. The commoners concede inferiority man to man, but deny it group to group. The reason? The public assembly collects perspectives as well as people; through the taking of counsel, fragmentary insights are composed into a rounded picture of the whole.

Was it true? In Aristotle's day, assemblies were often hard to tell from mobs. Today's representative legislatures are much less turbulent, but no more given to deliberation. Political scientists find that more is explained by the "aggregation of preferences" than the composition of insights. In fact, on most issues congressmen are too hyperspecialized even to have preferences. Instead of taking counsel, they take what political scientists call "cues" from colleagues whose hyperspecialties are different. Cue-taking would be all right if wisdom could be entirely reduced to technical expertise, but as the wise have taught, it cannot. The reason counsel itself is so rarely taken is that it is so demanding. In order for people to compose their scattered and one-sided insights, they must take counsel with firmness, fairness, coolness, discretion, and restraint. Most of all they must crave truth more than victory.

The compensation for defects of passion might be called *weaving*. The metaphor comes from Plato's *Statesman*, where the true man of state is portrayed as a weaver of opposite civic temperaments. The rash and the timid become the warp and woof of an intricate pattern in the fabric of the community. Plato is speaking not of composing fragmentary insights, but of tempering extremes of passion. Fear tempers fire, fire fear.

Weaving is an almost impossible discipline. Mix salty with bland and you get mulligatawny, but mix hawks with doves and you get mayhem. Now and then you may get a dove-hawk hybrid, but that is not much better, for though the mean and the midpoint are the same in arithmetic, they are different in policy: we should sometimes act and sometimes wait, sometimes spend and sometimes save, sometimes fight and sometimes flee. Therefore the weaving would also have to change with circumstance. It seems, then, that in order to weave successfully, the statesman himself must have virtue entire. To know how to manage souls he must be wise, just, moderate, and courageous himself.

In the end we see yet another application of the Hamburger Helper principle. Compensation does not replace virtue; it only extends its range. The taking of counsel composes insights only among those who have some virtue already. Weaving demands less virtue from the ruled, but even more from the rulers.

BALANCE

What of *balance*—that selfish groups be set against each other so that vice is checked and virtue given leverage? Achieving balance between opposing groups has generally been thought to involve three different tasks. First, the constitutional advantages of each group must be made as nearly equal as possible. Second, straddling every important cleavage, a middle or third group must be made as secure as possible. Third, incentives for opposing groups to court this middle must be established and strengthened.

Examples are easily compiled. The Few and the Many might be balanced by a middle class (Aristotle's theory), a monarch (the "literary" theory of England), an elected chief magistrate (John Adams's theory), or a college of magistrates (the "literary" theory of Rome). In similar fashion, opposing parties might be balanced by independent voters, opposing coalitions might be balanced by independent parties, a parliament and cabinet might be balanced by independent members, and so on.

Does balance solve the problem? One criticism, at least, is

groundless—that balance causes "gridlock," institutionalizing a bias in favor of an unjust status quo. This charge overlooks the role of the middle. As the English Reform Acts demonstrated, competition between the extremes in the presence of a middle can even supply a motive to make the middle bigger, to enfranchise portions of the population that have previously been excluded from full political rights.

Other charges against the strategy of constitutional balance are harder to dismiss. (1) The classical version of the strategy of balance told a story of the Many, the Few, and the Middle. Conflict more often occurs between different factions of the Few, variously allied with the Middle and variously mediated by the sullenness or compliance of the Many. The lower orders have less protection than the classical strategy supposes. Furthermore, (2) those who devise schemes to balance opposing groups are apt to be involved in the conflict themselves. Beyond this, (3) any device that can be used to weaken the strong and strengthen the weak, as balance requires, can also be used to strengthen the strong and weaken the weak. If the social positions of the groups to be balanced are grossly unequal, then (5) the middle group may even be exploited by the Few as a buffer against the Many—a scapegoat. In addition, (6) balanced government is complicated government. The more complicated the government, the more difficult to know whom to blame when something goes wrong. And (7), no matter how well groups are balanced, changes in their behavior over time are likely to knock them out of balance again. For instance the legislature, at first factious, wild, and impulsive, may later settle down, while judges, at first modest and steady, may become capricious and arrogant.

Problems of other sorts also arise. For example, (8) opposites can not only balance each other—they can also *provoke* each other, egging each other on to fly further and further from the mean. Moreover, (9) coalitions against the Middle do occasionally occur. The Roman senatorial elite was sometimes able to gain the support of the urban rabble for laws that hurt the middle class, and in America, incumbents of opposite parties, out to increase their own advantage, find common cause against challengers. Then again, (10) there are such things as unbalanceable groups. Although there may be none that *cannot* be taken into a constitutional scheme of balances, there are some that *should* not be. The Church, for instance, ought not to be made a "second estate"; it is a "colony of heaven," not a province of this world. Besides that, (11) just as there are some groups that should not be taken into a constitutional scheme of balance, so there are some issues that should not be resolved by compromise. For instance, the Middle cannot be right about abortion, because killing the child is either murderous or not.

In any case, (12) whatever device we use to even the scales between opposing groups is likely to generate a new opposition that is itself in need of balancing. Suppose we were to even up the rulers and the ruled by dividing the former into "branches." Horizontal collusion would become less important, but vertical collusion would become more. Thus in the United States, each interest group has its own little chunk of the civil service and the legislature.

In addition, (13) certain policies disturb the constitutional balance even though they contradict no constitutional rule. The classical example of a constitutional sleeper is the Roman policy of imperialism, which indirectly made free farming unprofitable on the Italian peninsula and thereby destroyed the landed middle class. For future historians, the classical example of a constitutional sleeper might be the welfare state, which *produces* classes which are dependent on the continuation of the regime.

Finally, (14) who really gains from what is often difficult to tell. For instance, a landed elite may like nothing better than to make the franchise universal, for tenants will probably accept direction from those on whom they are dependent. The real loser here is the middle class.

Considering these flaws, balance might still give us a *little* better than the government we deserve, but it cannot plausibly give us justice and good order in the complete absence of virtue. The most penetrating theorists of balance have understood this. Aristotle seemed to conceive the opposition of selfish groups not so much in terms of checking vice, as in terms of giving *leverage* to the otherwise voiceless group cast in the role of balancer. In his ideal case, the balancing group is really virtuous; all of the swing votes are held by "a few good men and true." In his second-best case, the balancer does not have virtue, but imitates it; all of the swing votes are held by members of the middle class, who are far from being saints yet have none of the usual motives for injustice. They are neither so rich that they can exploit their neighbors, nor so poor that they have nothing to lose by revolution.

CHANNELING

Next in our order of strategies comes *channeling*—in which nonvirtuous motives are shaped and directed so that they give rise to the same behavior to which virtue would give rise. Without noticing, we have considered an instance of channeling already. Remember that according to Aristotle the middle class is well cast to balance the Few against the Many not because it truly has virtue, but because it imitates it: its middling position shapes and directs its desire for security in just such fashion that it avoids both extremes of injustice.

For Aristotle, channeling is part of a broader strategy of balance. However, channeling can also work by itself. Desire for independence, for example, is no more a virtue than desire for security, but it imitates a virtue well enough to have fooled both Thomas Jefferson and Alexander Hamilton. Hence Hamilton, who found the desire for independence in business, pinned his political hopes on the leadership of gentlemen, whereas Jefferson, who found it in farming, pinned his on the sons of earth. From either point to policy is but a single step: for Jefferson, commerce is anathema, while for Hamilton, it is a republican necessity.

In principle, almost any motive might be the object of channeling. In our century, disastrous attempts have been made to put even envy, fear, and hatred into harness for the good. Republics, however, exploit a different set of motives. Our keenest republican theories of channeling can be credited to Augustine, Adam Smith, and Alexis de Tocqueville. Reflecting on the history of Rome, Augustine explained how the love of glory could prompt seemingly public-spirited deeds by keeping yet worse motives in check. Smith and Tocqueville developed similar analyses of the love of wealth. What makes these thinkers so acute is their recognition that successful channeling has both *institutional* and *moral* requirements. For the Augustinian strategy, the institutional requirements include, first, a society of fixed statuses, for only a nobility is interested in glory, and second, an arena of competition, for otherwise the glory motive would have no direction. Smith and Tocqueville require a society *without* fixed statuses, for only under a regime of insecurity are people sufficiently interested in gain. On the other hand, they too require an arena of competition, otherwise the gain motive would be similarly undirected.

The moral requirements are more interesting because they show that channeling is yet another Hamburger Helper strategy, like deterrence, filtration, compensation, and balance. Rather than offering a substitute for virtue, it seems, by a Faustian bargain, to make a little bit go further. Augustinian nobles must have not only a desire for glory but a sense of what truly merits it; Smithian entrepreneurs, not only a desire for gain but a sense of restraint; and Tocquevillian citizens, not only self-interest but "self-interest rightly understood." Otherwise, nobles are just as apt to seek fame by fraudulent means as by fair, following Machiavelli's advice that if they cannot be entirely good, they should be entirely evil. Otherwise, businessmen are just as apt to collude as to compete, following mercantilist advice to seek tariffs, privileges, and monopolies. Otherwise, citizens are just as apt to seek license as liberty, following demagogic advice to step on the faces of their fellows in order to rise.

Only Augustine, however, perceived the paradox that channeling entails. Channeling does not just manipulate the subvirtuous motives with which it deals; it *accommodates* them. This is like promising an alcoholic a drink for staying sober. For a while, then—a few centuries in the most successful cases—channeling seems to work. But in the long run it undermines that little bit of virtue that it seems to stretch; it saws off the limb that it is sitting on. Hence between the channeling of gain and glory and the channeling of fear and envy there may be less difference than we think. Sallust and Cicero, who do not know the difference between a virtue and its imitation, are at a loss to understand why *gloria* was supplanted by *cupiditas* and *ambitio* in Rome. Not Augustine; he knows. Do we?

INCULCATION

Inculcation means that, through law in the broadest sense, government tries to teach virtue directly. All of our substitutes for virtue have turned out to be merely unreliable ways to extend its range. Shall we use law in the broadest sense—not only its essential acts, commanding, permitting, and prohibiting, but also their modalities, such as honoring and dishonoring, encouraging and discouraging, protecting and attacking, helping and hindering, declaring and denying, giving and taking, educating and administering—to make men good?

We know at least that the law cannot be neutral. Everything a government does is founded on some understanding of what is good. Moreover, no law that has effect at all can fail to have effect on character. On the other hand, granted that the law must take an interest in whether men are becoming worse or better, it does not follow that it must *make* men better. Perhaps it is a *poor* teacher; other teachers are better, and it only hinders them when it tries to do their job. The position I maintain is threefold: It *is;* they *are;* and it *does.* Hence, a fitter set of maxims than "Make men better" is "Protect the true teachers of virtue; get out of their way; and be sure not to make men *worse.*" The true teachers are church and family.

The state should defer to church and family partly because of its own nature. Though government exists for the common good, it is the target of partisan interests. Capture by these interests is just as easy when it tries to teach as when it tries to tax. Consider, for example, the present struggle over whether sodomy is to be legitimized as a way of life. As both armies engaged in the struggle understand, this war concerns the distribution not only of privileges but of esteem: rules concerning adoption, employment, housing, and health are just as "educational" as rules concerning what is to be taught in the public schools.

Now despite the risk of partisan capture, the government *must* do what no one else can do. But others do raise children and minister to souls. The family is not subject to partisan capture at all; normal parents love their children as no politician can, and they do not stand for election. The visible Church is subject to capture, but unlike the government, it is purely voluntary.

The state should also defer to church and family because of the nature of moral development. We often speak as though becoming good were an arithmetic process of adding good qualities and subtracting bad ones, so that the greater the sum, the better we get, and we can get just as good as we please. But for three reasons, this picture is false to human experience.

One reason is the Paradox of the Treacherous Good: bad qualities always depend on *imperfectly* good ones for their vigor; the more of the good ones we have, the more harm we can do with the bad ones. We all know that patience and caution are good qualities; but unless we are speaking of that *perfected* patience which awaits only good and of that *perfected* caution which fears only evil, then these qualities may serve knaves as well as honest men. A man must be not only taught and trained, but *turned around.* He must repent.

Another reason is the Paradox of Elevation: because we imitate virtue by channeling vices, apparent improvement in a single moral dimension can mask the fact that in the long run one is getting worse in all of them. A climber may be going in the wrong direction even though the ground is rising on the path he walks. Consider, in its nobler forms, the vice of pride. It may demand obsequies—but at least it never offers them. It may step on unrelated inferiors — but it is generous to its dependents. It may make evil vows—but whatever its vows, it keeps them. Eventually it poisons the springs of all the virtues—but, most glorious of banes, on its tainted way it achieves some mighty splendors. All of this deceives us. A man must be not only turned around, but turned in the *right direction.* He needs the word of God.

The third reason is the Paradox of Countervailing Vice: the cure of a channeled vice may open the door to others that are even worse. We have seen the Hoover Dams of channeling already. Vice dons virtue in smaller ways as well; for instance, the need to condescend, or the urge to atone, may ape compassion for the weak and misused. Unfortunately, if weeds and wheat are matted together, a yank on one may uproot the other. Chide glory, and the nobility grow slothful. Curb materialism, and the merchants grow indolent. Cure condescension and displacement of guilt, and the compassionate grow indifferent. A man must be not only turned around and turned aright, but *transformed.* He needs God's grace.

Repentance, revelation, and grace are far beyond the scope of law. That is the doom of official inculcation.

SUBSIDIARITY

Through *subsidiarity,* government honors virtue and protects its teachers, but without attempting to take their place. We reach this strategy by tumbling out of the former one; the arguments that pull us into subsidiarity are the same ones that pushed us out of inculcation. But we must be careful not to misunderstand where we have gotten. In the first place, the fact that subsidiarity is opposed to inculcation in no way makes it neutral. A state that defers to parents and church has not thereby suspended judgment; it has judged *with* them that their jobs are not its own. A state that forgoes inculcation has not thereby denied its own influence on character; it has agreed that it ought not to put this influence in competition with that of parents and church. A state that lays down its pretension to make men good has not thereby abandoned concern for their goodness; it has merely removed the chief cause of its making them worse. Subsidiarity means confirming good qualities taught elsewhere—instead of tearing them up and replacing them.

The second point we must be careful not to misunderstand is what it means to "protect" the family and the church—what it means for the state to be a *subsidium,* a help. Concerning the family, G. K. Chesterton put the problem well in *The Well and the Shadows.* What he disliked most, he said, "is not the Communist attacking the family or the Capitalist betraying the family; it is the vast and very astonishing vision of the Hitlerite defending the family. Hitler's way of defending the independence of the family is to make every family dependent on him and his semi-Socialist State; and to preserve the authority of parents by authoritatively telling all the parents what to do. . . . In other words, he appears to interfere with family life more even than the Bolshevists do; and to do it in the name of the sacredness of the family." This sort of thing does not require death camps or wars of conquest; it gets along better without them. All it needs is the quiet, crushing kindness of the welfare state. Government first taxes away the family income, then "helps" the families thereby enfeebled by giving back part of the income in the form of "benefits" and regulations that further reduce their independence and vitality. Schools, for instance, are "free," but parents cannot choose their children's teachers or control what their children will be taught. "When they come through that door," said an education despot in the seat of government, "they're mine."

The point I am making concerns the Church as well. Not only does the modern state interfere with family in the name of family, it interferes with faith in the name of faith. Whenever it is not scolding the church in fear of her challenge, it is whispering to her in hopes of making her pregnant with its purposes. So intent on seducing the Bride of Christ is Mr. Clinton, still President at the time of writing, that during his candidacy he tried to imitate her Husband's voice. Identifying himself with the Redeemer, he called his program the New Covenant, then misquoted Scripture to support it: "No eye has seen, no ear has heard, no mind has imagined *what we can build*," he prophesied at his convention. The way this runs in Scripture itself is, "No eye has seen, no ear has heard, no mind has conceived *what God has prepared for those who love him*." (1 Cor. 2:9, NIV, quoting Isa. 64:4). The biblical passage gives sovereignty to God. Although the President's language still sounds biblical, it gives sovereignty to Man.

Subsidiarity, then, does not mean that the state flatters, seduces, or absorbs the true teachers of virtue. It means it gets out of their way, and keeps other things from getting in their way. The state gets out of the way not by raising taxes and putting all mothers on the dole, but by reducing taxes so that they do not have to work; not by making sex a compulsory subject in the schools, but by letting families choose their own schools; not by keeping children from ever hearing a public prayer, but by keeping them from ever hearing a public obscenity; not by calling for a "politics of meaning," but by honoring that Meaning which no politics made, that Glory which even the heavens, though soulless, declare.

Is subsidiarity, then, a solution to the problem? No. But until the world is remade, we can probably do no better.

5

The Problem with Communitarianism

WHAT IS ONE TO MAKE OF COMMUNITARIANISM? For a
Christian, answering this question presents no small
difficulty. Certainly Christians have no difficulty with
community *as such*. At the core of our faith is the salvation story,
and it turns out that without the notion of a people or nation—
without the concept of a group of human beings that share a way of
life and agree about ultimate loyalties—the story cannot even be
told. The problem lies in which community one is speaking about.

The briefest summary of the salvation story as it has been passed
down to us will make this clear. In the earliest times we human
beings, made by God in His image for intimacy with Himself and
with one another, ruined ourselves beyond all human means of cure
by seeking autonomy instead. Even so, He took initiative to redeem
us. From all the nations, He drew one nation apart to be His own:
"Has any god ever tried to take for himself one nation out of another
nation, by testings, by miraculous signs and wonders, by war, by a
mighty hand and an outstretched arm, or by great and awesome deeds,
like all the things the Lord your God did for you in Egypt before
your very eyes? You were shown these things so that you might

know that the Lord is God; besides him there no other" (Deut. 4:34-35). From this nation God promised to raise a suffering servant and messianic king, who would not only fulfill God's promises to it but also offer redemption to the other nations. Through the prophet Isaiah, God says to this savior: "It is too small a thing for you to be my servant to restore the tribes of Jacob and bring back those of Israel I have kept. I will also make you a light for the Gentiles [literally, other nations], that you may bring my salvation to the ends of the earth" (Isa. 49:6). This savior was Jesus, who bore the sins of the people according to prophecy. After his resurrection, first telling his followers that all authority in heaven and on earth had been given to him, he commanded them to "go and make disciples of all nations" (Matt. 28:18-19). Thus, through the action of the Holy Spirit, the people of promise have entered a radically new phase that will end only with the Messiah's return. "There is neither Jew nor Greek, slave nor free, male nor female, for you are all one in Christ Jesus. If you belong to Christ, then you are Abraham's seed, and heirs according to the promise" (Gal. 3:28-29). Although the members of the redeemed community are to respect earthly governors and human institutions, their former commonwealths can no longer command their final allegiance: "Many are enemies of the cross of Christ. . . . Their mind is on earthly things. But our citizenship is in heaven" (Phil. 3:18, 19b, 20a).

You see the problem. The temporal community—my school, my club, my town, my nation, or what have you—does surround me with neighbors, each of whom is a matter of transcendent consequence. Moreover this community does occasion genuine duties, for God has commanded my submission to legitimate authority. Because of this—because the temporal City is an unwitting backdrop for a great drama—what goes on within it does matter to the Christian. But the temporal City is not the eternal City. The pageantry and shadow play of its patriotic songs and rituals all trade on a longing for that which no earthly commonwealth can satisfy; they seduce the citizen with words and tokens that are really native to another clime. So in the final analysis, every community but one, the community of faith, is merely external. And although this Commonwealth transcends all old communal lines, it does so only for those who enter within its gates. All of these facts put the Christian sharply at odds with any program to make the temporal community the starting point for ethical or political theory—if that is what communitarianism is. That which is secular is not thereby neutral.

Another way to explore the difficulty with "communitarianism" is to point out that there are at least three communitarianisms, each of which poses problems of its own. The *demonic* variety makes the community itself the source of value; the *accountable* variety submits the community to values of which it is not the source, but which can be identified by all; and the *narrative* variety submits it to values of which it is not the source, but which *cannot* be identified by all. Let us briefly consider each in turn.

DEMONIC AND ACCOUNTABLE COMMUNITARIANISM

First, demonic communitarianism, the discredited ideology of the *Volk* or People that was epitomized by Adolf Hitler and Joseph Goebbels. It was an idolatry, which like all idolatries eventually demanded sacrifices of blood. By treating the community itself as the source of value and the criterion of truth, the Nazis opened vaults of wickedness so vast that they have hardly yet been fathomed. Yet the problem was not chiefly that the Nazis were monsters. It was that their theory of value *makes* monsters of all who live it to its logical conclusion, be they angry German socialists or merely clever American relativists. Christians have a special responsibility to guard against the demonic sort of communitarianism, because the last time it raised its head its pagan proponents mounted a concerted effort to put a false Christian face on it. They knew that lies can become powerful only in the disguise of truths.

Second, accountable communitarianism, represented by Amitai Etzioni and the authors of the *Responsive Communitarian Platform*. While stressing the importance of communal integrity, they firmly deny that community *as such* is the criterion of truth, or that values become good "merely because such values originate in a community." Therefore, they declare, "communal values must be judged by external and overriding criteria, based on shared human experience."

The problem is that when put to the test, these accountable communitarians decline to render such judgment. For after urging that schools provide moral education, they answer the question "Whose morals are you going to teach?" with the simple statement that "We ought to teach those values Americans share"—"for example, that the dignity of all persons ought to be respected, that tolerance is a virtue and discrimination is abhorrent, that peaceful resolution of conflicts is superior to violence, that generally truth-telling is superior to lying, that democratic government is morally superior to totalitarianism and authoritarianism, that one ought to give a day's work for a day's pay, that saving for one's own and one's country's future is better than squandering one's income and relying on others to attend to one's future needs."

The presupposition behind the counsel to teach the values that Americans share is presumably that American values do pass the test of external and overriding criteria based on shared human experience. But this is not obviously true. Most of the values on the list reflect not so much external and overriding criteria based on shared human experience as a watery compromise among our warring political subcultures. Giving meaning to these glittering generalities requires making specific commitments that the *Platform* avoids. One wonders if the authors of the *Platform* themselves agree about whether the "dignity of all persons" is offended by abortion, whether racial quotas honor or violate the principle that "discrimination is abhorrent," or whether the virtue of "tolerance" requires putting up with obscenity in the music of rock and rap. Consider, too, the values left *off* the list. Not even the American people themselves seem completely at ease about whether their admitted obsessions with sexual pleasure and material possession meet the test of external and overriding criteria. But this unease does not make them any less obsessions; they remain "values Americans share."

Now so far, the worst one could say about accountable communitarianism is that it has not taken its premises to their logical conclusion. It needs to *declare* the external and overriding criteria, based on shared human experience, that its qualified defense of communities requires; it needs something like natural law. But here we find ourselves in an extraordinary predicament. Natural law is far from unproblematic itself, and communitarianism is often regarded as a maneuver for getting around its mysteries rather than entering into them. Making matters worse is that although natural law is widely (and somewhat misleadingly*) considered a Christian doctrine, Christians often find it no less mysterious than others do. Because we are here engaged in defining a Christian response to communitarianism, let us investigate this mystery. Not until we do so will we be in a position to consider the third kind of communitarianism.

The earliest antecedents of natural law theory are all pagan, from Antigone's appeal to a law that surpasses the king's decree, to Aristotle's distinction between natural justice and merely conventional justice, to the Stoic doctrine of a law of nature proper.

Scripture, one might think, would say more, for it testifies that God is the Creator, and surely His purposes would be reflected in His creation. In fact it says very little about the subject. Scripture declares God's message in plain words. If one has that, what need has one to scan the hieroglyph of nature? The Old Testament has no term for "nature" at all. The New Testament does, but uses it in a

---

* Misleadingly, because Christians consider it part of "general" revelation—given not only to Christians but to the whole human race.

ordinary moral sense only once; this usage is found in a passage (Rom. 1:26-27) contrasting natural with unnatural sexual relations (that which is *phusikán* with that which is *para phusin*). As to natural law proper, only once in all of Scripture are we told that anything of the sort exists. Even here it is mentioned only parenthetically, by way of explaining how it is that unconverted Gentiles, who have neither waited at the foot of Sinai nor sat at the feet of Jesus, can be responsible for their sins at all. Paul says: "Indeed, when Gentiles, who have not the law, do by nature (*phusei*) the things required by the law, they are a law for themselves, even though they do not have the law, since they show that the requirements of the law are written on their hearts, their consciences also bearing witness, and their thoughts now accusing, now even defending them" (Rom. 2:14-15).

Just how much of the requirements of the law *is* written on the human heart? This is sometimes questioned, for whatever the heart's original condition, both Testaments make clear that its present condition is abnormal. Jeremiah proclaims (17:9) that "The heart is deceitful above all things and beyond cure. Who can understand it?" Paul reminds the Ephesians that before the experience of transforming grace, both he and they lived among the disobedient, "gratifying the cravings of our sinful nature (*epithumiais tás sarkos*, 'strong passions of the flesh') and following its desires and thoughts." "Like the rest," he says, "we were by nature (*phusei*) objects of wrath" (Eph. 2:3). He further holds that persistence in sin darkens or perverts even what natural knowledge there is:

> For since the creation of the world God's invisible qualities— his eternal power and divine nature—have been clearly seen, being understood from what has been made, so that men are without excuse. For although they knew God, they neither glorified him as God nor gave thanks to him, but their thinking became futile and their foolish hearts were darkened. . . . Furthermore, since they did not think it worthwhile to retain the knowledge of God, he gave them over to a depraved mind,

to do what ought not to be done. . . . [T]hey invent ways of doing evil. . . . [A]lthough they know God's righteous decree that those who do such things deserve death, they not only continue to do these very things but also approve of those who practice them (Rom. 1:20-21,28,30,32).

Christians have understood these passages in a variety of ways. Thomas Aquinas sometimes seemed to speak as though the mind had not fallen as far as the rest of human nature; more exactly, he held that the damage of sin lay not so much in the faculty of reason itself as in its ability to regulate the passions. Thus he saw no obstacle to the development of a complete doctrine of natural law, which could be common ground even between Christians and unbelievers.

If natural law doctrine did provide such a common ground, the accountable communitarians would truly have the "external and overriding criteria, based on shared human experience" that they desire. Catholics and some others say it does. More than that, within the doctrine of natural law they would have an explicit doctrine of community itself. As Pius XI declared in 1931 in *Quadragesimo anno* ("On Reconstructing the Social Order"): "Just as it is gravely wrong to take from individuals what they can accomplish by their own initiative and industry and give it to the community, so also it is an injustice and at the same time a grave evil and disturbance of right order to assign to a greater and higher association what lesser and subordinate organizations can do. For every social activity ought of its very nature to furnish help (*subsidium*) to the members of the body social, and never destroy or absorb them."

The principle of subsidiarity is *pro-community*, but *anti-collectivist*. Those who propose a communitarian alternative to the liberal state would do well to give it close consideration. Its basis is the honor due to persons on account of their being made in the image of God. To be sure, there is a hierarchy of human organizations from families right on up to the central government—but this is a hierarchy of scale and power, not of dignity or resemblance to the Al-

mighty. To be sure, there is such a thing as supra-personal solidar-
ity—but the Church, not the state, is called the Body of Christ, and
the only union to have sacramental existence besides the Church is
the union of husband and wife. To be sure, we are to lose ourselves—
but in face-to-face service to persons who are known to God by
name, not in thralldom to impersonal abstractions that are known to
nobody. Nothing that families can do for each other should be taken
away by associations; nor anything that associations can do, by government; nor anything that local governments can do, by that vast
power at the center.

   But we are getting ahead of ourselves. I said that different Christians understood the Scriptures on human nature in different ways.
We have spoken of Catholic Christians; what about the others? By
contrast with thinkers like Thomas Aquinas, the most radical of the
Reformers thought a normative doctrine of natural law deeply prob-
lematic. In the first place, they held, the corruption of the passions
would make it impossible for even a perfect human mind to trace
the original intentions of the Creator. In the second place, the lapsed
human mind is no longer perfect; sin has twisted the faculty of reason at least as much as it has the passions. That which is written on
the human heart may be sufficient to generate consciousness of guilt—
Paul meant no more—but it is surely insufficient either to guide or
to motivate.

   This bleak interpretation left the Reformers but two possibilities for the project of developing a normative doctrine of natural
law. One was to develop a *new kind,* by reasoning not *backwards* to
creation but *forwards* from the Fall. Of course, both kinds of doctrine draw attention to what we share by being human. But whereas
the older theorists of natural law drew attention to the pattern that
was broken, the newer ones drew attention to the brokenness of the
pattern; whereas the former asked, "What clues to the divine design
have *survived* the corruption of human nature?", the latter asked
"What follows from the *bare fact* that human nature is corrupt?"

This project left much to be desired, for the new theorists of natural law never explained why a mind that was too corrupt to answer the former question was not also too corrupt to answer the latter. Nor did they succeed in banishing all assumptions about the proper ordering of human desires. Thomas Hobbes tacitly made a *summum bonum* of the desire to live, while Samuel Pufendorf tacitly made one of the desire for sociality.

The other possibility was to give up natural law and rely on Scripture alone, trusting the grace of God to hold the wayward mind steady in the effort to understand it. There is much to be said for this, and it remains the choice of many evangelicals. But that brings us to the third kind of communitarianism.

NARRATIVE COMMUNITARIANISM

Can external and overriding criteria for judgment based on shared human experience be identified to the satisfaction of all by *any* means—whether of the old or the new understanding of natural law? Narrative communitarianism says crisply: No.

To be sure, narrative communitarians admit that there may be such a thing as shared human experience. The problem, as they see it, is that the only resource any particular human being has for *interpreting* his shared experience is the tale his community tells of itself—whether a story of Exodus, of Revolution, of Death and Resurrection, or of Poor Boys Making Good. Whichever it is, this story does several things. First, it tells how life should be lived and identifies the proper object of unconditioned loyalty, be this object God, Success, or the Classless Society. Second, it sets the boundaries of the community, because it shapes those who enter into the story in a way that others who hear it cannot be shaped. Boundaries remain boundaries even when others are invited to cross them and make the story theirs, for not all will accept such an invitation. According to narrative communitarians, the lesson of these boundaries is stark and immutable: *That which makes sense of shared experience is not itself a shared experience; that which makes common humanity intelligible is not itself common to all humanity.*

On this view, even natural law would be viewed as merely a part of some community's story. This can be said of either of the forms of natural law. How can it be said of the old? Asked for his scriptural authority, Thomas Aquinas would have cited Paul's remark about the law that is written even on the hearts of the Gentiles. But Paul was a Pharisee, trained by Rabbi Gamaliel in both oral and written Jewish Law. Thus he may have been thinking of the rabbinic tradition of a Noahide Law, different from the Mosaic Law in being written on the hearts of all of Noah's descendants—the whole human race—rather than being proclaimed to Israel alone. This tradition was itself a *mishnah* on Genesis 6:5-19:19, a story of wickedness, flood, and deliverance.

And how can it be said of the new natural law? Asked for *their* scriptural authority, Hobbes and Pufendorf would have gone directly to another story, the story of the Fall in Genesis 3, perhaps including the ensuing violence of Cain against Abel in Genesis 4:1-9. From this they would have abstracted the idea of a pre-political state of anarchy and confusion, ended, through social contract, by the civil state. For them the natural law is nothing but the prudential theorems that follow from the conditions in which the contract originates.

In each case, the narrative communitarian would claim, the idea of moral principles that are recognized among all mankind is rooted in a story that is *not* recognized among all mankind. His claim would be that without some such story such moral principles are mere regularities rather than law and too thin to be of service in the very predicaments where we need them most.

Driven by such reflections, some narrative communitarians wander into a sort of relativism that leaves them defenseless against communitarians of the first, demonic, sort. The Alasdair MacIntyre of *After Virtue* is perhaps the most brilliant example of a thinker in this predicament.* In better shape, I suggest, are the theologians Stanley Hauerwas and his colleague William H. Willimon, who are often classified as communitarians but prefer to be called simply Christians. Unlike communitarians proper, they recognize something crucial: the impossibility of passing purely human judgment on communal stories from a vantage point somewhere outside them does not preclude the possibility that a particular story is, simply, true, and that God might have provided the means for humans to know it. In fact they do claim truth for their own story—which, in a very un-modern but very Christian sort of universalism, they invite the participants in the other stories to join. Disconcerting those who still cling to the withered dugs of the Enlightenment, they blazon in *Resident Aliens* that "any political slogan that does not need God to make itself credible" is suspect. "Apart from the life and

---

* How MacIntyre's later work should be characterized is by no means clear. For example, although *Three Rival Versions of Moral Enquiry* is sometimes viewed as having vindicated a particular narrative, that is not what MacIntyre himself says about it. He does hold that the "rational superiority" of what he calls "tradition" over what he calls "genealogy" might "in due time" be demonstrated. However, he not only denies having accomplished such a demonstration, but says that the time for it is "not yet due." On closer consideration it seems that the time might never fall due, because his criterion for rational superiority is that one viewpoint can show that another fails *in its own terms and by its own standards*—a criterion which seems to hold every critic hostage to the bad faith of his opponents' terms and standards. Even what MacIntyre means by "tradition" seems to vary: it can be singular (the tradition of Thomas Aquinas), plural (the Aristotelian and Augustinian traditions which Thomas Aquinas unified), or generic (any tradition which, like these, satisfies criteria which make participants conversationally accountable to one another). Finally, although MacIntyre recognizes that every actual tradition depends on some conception of a truth beyond and ordering all particular truths, he nowhere says (1) that any such conception is correct, (2) that a demonstration of the rational superiority of its corresponding tradition would vindicate it, or even (3) that it could be vindicated.

death of Jesus of Nazareth," they explain, the Church "really does not know" the meaning of abstractions like peace and justice.

My own position is that of a Christian believer in natural law of the classical sort who finds himself much closer to the Hauerwasian stance than Christian natural law theorists of the classical sort usually do. On the tablets of the heart a law is indeed written, the same for all men—as Thomas Aquinas said—not only as to rectitude but as to knowledge. But it is a far cry from knowing something to acknowledging it, and the human race has been in the condition that psychologists call "denial" ever since the Fall.

Denial is no modern discovery; Thomas himself recognizes it. He divides the precepts of the natural law into categories: primary, or general principles, and secondary, or detailed principles. It seems that when reason is perverted, the secondary principles *can* be blotted out of the heart—as it were, forgotten. Thomas lists five ways in which such perversion can occur. Reason can be perverted by *passion* as when, momentarily blinded by grief and rage, I unjustly strike the bearer of the news that my wife is deep in adultery with another man. Reason can be perverted by *evil habit* as when, little by little, I get into the habit of using pornography or cutting corners on my taxes. At first, my conscience bothers me, but eventually I see nothing wrong with my behavior. Reason can be perverted by *evil disposition of nature* as when, by defect in one of my chromosomes, I suffer a genetic predisposition to alcoholism. I am still capable of restraint, but it is more difficult for me than it might be for another. Reason can be perverted by *vicious custom* as when, having grown up among people who do not regard bribery as wrong, I take it for granted. Finally, reason can be perverted by *evil persuasion* as when, justifying my behavior on the theory that I am merely exploiting the exploiters, I use electronic tricks to make free long-distance telephone calls. Another name for evil persuasion might be "depraved ideology."

Although the primary precepts cannot be simply forgotten as the secondary precepts can be, even the primary precepts can be blotted out from the heart in "particular actions"—that is, misapplied. A pair of illustrations will make this distinction clear. Consider the precept against raiding a neighboring tribe. According to Thomas, this precept is secondary; I can forget it, as Julius Caesar wrote that the ancient Germans had forgotten it. They knew theft was wrong, but they did not recognize raiding as theft.* Contrast the precept against the taking of innocent human life. This precept is primary; I cannot forget it without ceasing to be human altogether. But I can rationalize. I can say, "Yes, but the bastard I killed wasn't innocent!" In the same way, I can tell myself that the unborn child whose blood I shed was not human, or that it was not alive. One of the most remarkable phenomena of our century is the rise of entire political movements devoted to the rationalization of particular sins. Paul could have explained this to us; to those who are determined to make themselves stupid, God says, "Your will be done." (Paraphrasing Romans 1:28.)

To be sure, at some level I pay a price for my rationalizations. Denial takes up so much psychological energy that eventually something has to give. For instance, women in literally thousands of recovery groups report symptoms of Post-Abortion Stress Syndrome: the symptoms vary from case to case and take different amounts of time to appear, but commonly include depression, anxiety, inability to bond with wanted children, resentment of other women's children, and many other indications of distress. Yet whether we pay a price for our rationalizations or not, the fact remains that we can rationalize. Instruction in ethics is no remedy; the more we know, the better we are at it. The lesson I draw from this is that to *profess* moral truths, even when they are not only universally valid but even,

---

* Because of the ambiguity of Thomas's language, some interpreters have thought he meant that the Germans had actually forgotten the precept against theft. This could not be his meaning, for elsewhere he makes clear that the prohibition of theft is one of those "general" precepts known at some level to all.

in some sense, universally known, cannot be a theologically neutral act. It will inevitably be tied—to a story.

Now the polity is not a community in the simple sense, but a community of communities; not a hearth, but a vestibule. That means that many stories contend. Two things follow. First, any "communitarianism" feasible for the polity as a whole could be reached only by tactical mutual accommodation; second, it could be reached only among those communities whose stories were sufficiently related for them to find some common ground. For instance Catholics, Eastern Orthodox, Evangelical Protestants, and religious Jews might be able to reach such an accommodation. One could say in this case that they had agreed about the precepts of the natural law.

The problem is that secular humanists have their own "communitarianism"—a counter-accommodation, involving different groups, with different stories, sharing a different common ground—and these two communitarianisms are utterly at odds. In order to know which ground one can occupy, one must decide whose story is true. There is no other way.

6

The Problem with Liberalism

BELIEVERS IN THE CONGREGATION OF MY YOUTH took for
granted that Christianity and liberal politics were opposed.
The Bible seemed to back them up. Of Lyndon Johnson's
two great wars, for instance, they viewed the first, the war in Viet-
nam, with enthusiasm because America was a "City upon a Hill,"
while viewing the other, the war on poverty, with indifference because "the poor will always be with us." An antiwar socialist, I re-
belled, eventually leaving the faith completely. When in middle
adulthood I returned, I found myself in a congregation of a different
kind. Here, to my surprise, the believers took for granted that Christianity and liberal politics were brothers. Again Scripture was gleaned
for support: "Inasmuch as ye have done it unto one of the least of
these my brethren, ye have done it unto me"—obvious backing for
the welfare state; "There is neither male nor female, for ye are all one
in Christ Jesus"—a manifesto for feminism; "God is love, and he
that dwelleth in love dwelleth in God, and God in him"—homosexual activists asked for no more. As a teenager I had hurled some
of the same verses at my elders. God had devised a cunning pen-
ance.

Of course, both sides were tearing passages out of context and reading into them things that are not there. The City upon a Hill is the Body of Christ, not the United States of America. If the poor will always be with us, then we will always have to care for them. I am expected to look after the least of Christ's brethren myself, not to have the government send them checks. The apostle who said that in Him there is no male or female also said that in the family their roles are different. And the apostle who said that God is love also claimed for God the authority to define His love.

Unfortunately, knowing these things does not answer the ideological question. Should Christians be political liberals? Or even, to put the query the other way around, can they be?

In one way, both forms of the question are wrong-headed. According to the letter to the Philippians, our commonwealth is in Heaven, not on earth. In the same vein, the Great Commission shows that the mission of the Church to the world is to preach the gospel, not to prop up any worldly regime or ideology. Therefore the primary identity of the Christian is in Christ—it cannot be in liberalism, any more than it can be in conservatism, communism, or communitarianism.

But to stop at this truth would be evasive. Although the faith does not mandate any worldly regime or generate any worldly ideology, it does stand in judgment upon worldly regimes and ideologies. Moreover, Scripture makes clear that so long as human institutions do not defy God's commandments, we are to submit to them. Under a monarchy, submission might mean nothing more than obedience. In a republic, however, submission includes participation, so we have no alternative but to take positions on political questions. Willy-nilly, this involves us in responding to the worldly philosophies by which other people settle such questions.

The result? Even though I am not a duck, I will sometimes seem to quack like a duck. I cannot be a liberal and I cannot even be in strategic alliance with liberals, but I may from time to time find myself in tactical alliance with them—just as with conservatives—defending the cause of particular laws, precepts, or policies that they too approve, but for reasons of their own. To keep my head, I had better be clear about what those reasons are and how they differ from mine. So although we cannot ask whether Christians can or should be political liberals, we can and should ask what Christians are to think of liberalism.

At the threshold of the question we run into another problem: The term "political liberalism" can mean several things. Its principal meanings are threefold. Broadly, it means constitutional government with a representative legislature and generous liberties. In political economy, it means a competitive, self-regulating market with minimal government interference. Colloquially, it means the contemporary variety of government-driven social reformism. The first sense makes liberals of both the *New Republic* and the *National Review*. The second makes the latter liberal, but not the former. The third makes the former liberal, but not the latter. For present purposes I use the term in the third sense.

My thesis is that, even as worldly philosophies go, political liberalism is deeply flawed. We may best describe it as a bundle of acute moral errors, with political consequences that grow more and more alarming as these errors are taken closer and closer to their logical conclusions. I am not speaking of such errors as celebrating sodomy and abortion—for these are merely symptoms—but of their causes. Nor am I speaking of all their causes—for this would require reading hearts—but of their intellectual causes. I am not even speaking of all their intellectual causes—for these are too numerous—but of the most obvious. No claim is here made that every political liberal commits all the moral errors all the time. Nor do I claim that all the moral errors are logically compatible, so they even could be all committed all the time. Certain moral errors support certain others, but others are at odds, so they must be committed selectively. One must not expect logical coherence in moral confusion.

The political implications of the faith are more negative than positive, so rejecting liberalism does not mean accepting conservatism. In the first place, under the influence of a liberal culture conservatives often fall for liberal moral errors too. In the second place, like every worldly ideology conservatism commits heresies of its own. But we can study conservatism in chapter seven.

PROPITIATIONISM

The first moral error of political liberalism is *propitiationism*. According to this notion I should do unto others as they want; according to Christianity I should do unto others as they need. Numerous mental habits contribute to the propitiationist frame of mind. Most of my college students, for instance, think "need" and "want" are just synonyms. Many also construe the Jeffersonian right to pursue happiness as a right to be made happy by the government. Propitiationism corresponds to a style of politics in which innumerable factions, both organized and unorganized, compete to become government clientele, fighting not only for shares of the public purse (such as grants and loan guarantees) but also for governmental preferences (such as trade barriers and racial quotas) and for official marks of esteem (such as multiculturalist curricula and recognition of homosexual unions). Of course, in a representative system every government functionary, whether liberal or not, finds it difficult to resist group pressures. Propitiationism, however, reinforces the habit of giving in by making capitulation a moral duty.

Christians can slip into propitiationism by misunderstanding the Golden Rule. This happens when we read *Do unto others as you would have them do unto you* as though it implied *Do unto others as they would have you do unto them*: "I would want others to honor my demands, so I should honor theirs." The mistake lies in overlooking the fact that the "you" to whom the precept is addressed is a free subject of the kingdom of heaven, not a stranger. We are therefore speaking of what *in Christ* we would have others do unto us—to minister to our godly needs, not to our foolish or sinful wants. Unto others we should minister in the same way. It follows that keeping the Golden Rule may even mean saying "No" or suggesting a better way. Jesus instructs us to feed the poor, and so we should; but Paul says to the church at Thessalonica, "For even when we were with you, this we commanded you, that if any would not work, neither should he eat."

To be sure, it is easier to see the need to say "No" to a greedy industrialist who wants the government to protect him from honest competition than to a teen mother who wants to marry the government instead of a man. Both want what is bad for them, yet he is likely to get much more of what he wants but does not need than she is. The sloppy sort of compassionator is tempted to say, "If he gets what isn't good for him, then it's only fair that she should get what isn't good for her." But to give it to her might be to take her sole beatitude away. Find another way to help her.

EXPROPRIATIONISM

The second moral error of political liberalism is *expropriationism*. According to this notion I may take from others to help the needy, giving nothing of my own; according to Christianity I should give of my own to help the needy, taking from no one. We might call expropriationism the Robin Hood fallacy. Today, the expropriationist is usually a propitiationist too, confusing the needy with some sub-set of the merely wanty. So we are speaking of a style of politics in which the groups in power decide for us which of their causes our wealth is to support, taking that wealth by force.

Many Christians seem to miss the point, thinking that expro-priation is wrong just because the wrong groups are in power, choos-ing the wrong causes for subsidy. This is where the horror stories are offered, and horrible they are: subsidies to promote abortion, subsidies to photograph crucifixes in jars of urine, subsidies for all sorts of wickedness and blasphemy. But expropriation would be wrong even if each of its causes were good. Consider the following progression:

1. On a dark street, a man draws a knife and demands my money for drugs.

2. Instead of demanding my money for drugs, he demands it for the Church.

3. Instead of being alone, he is with a bishop of the Church who acts as bagman.

4. Instead of drawing a knife, he produces a policeman who says I must do as he says.

5. Instead of meeting me on the street, he mails me his demand as an official agent of the government.

If the first is theft, it is difficult to see why the other four are not also theft. Expropriation is wrong not because its causes are wrong, but because it is a violation of the Eighth Commandment: Thou shalt not steal.

But how, one may ask, can *government* steal? We live in a republic; aren't we therefore just taking from ourselves? No, not even in a republic are the rulers identical with the ruled; nor for that matter are the ruled identical with each other. If we were just taking from ourselves, there would be no need for the taking to be enforced. Then is it wrong for government to tax at all? No, government may certainly collect taxes for the support of its proper work; that work, however, is not the support of all good causes, but merely punishing wrongdoers and commending rightdoers (1 Pet. 2:13-14). This establishes a strong presumption against all the other things into which government likes to stick its fingers; under no circumstances may they be considered part of its appointed task.

If government were to end its subsidy of good causes, wouldn't these good causes suffer? Not necessarily; they might even thrive. Marvin Olasky has shown in *The Tragedy of American Compassion* that government subsidy itself can make good causes suffer, for in taking money by force one weakens both the means and the motive for people to give freely. Not only that, government usually distorts good causes in the act of absorbing them. But what if the causes did depend on the proceeds of theft? Should we do evil, that good may come? When some people accused Paul of teaching this doctrine, he called the charge a slander. There is no such thing as a tame sin that will do only what we want it to, going quietly back into its bottle when we have finished with it. Sin is no more like that than God is. In politics, no less than in private life, it ramifies.

SOLIPSISM

The third moral error of political liberalism is *solipsism*. According to this notion human beings make themselves, belong to themselves, and have value in and of themselves; according to Christianity they are made by God, belong to Him, and have value because they are loved by Him and made in His image. "Your eyes shall be opened," said the serpent, "and ye shall be as gods." Solipsism holds that we already are.

Political liberalism was not always explicitly solipsistic, but the change has hardly been noticed. John Locke in 1688 and Immanuel Kant in 1797 both held that we are not to use others merely as means to our ends. And yet though one can read in many books that they were saying the same thing, Locke gives as his reason that we are here to serve God's ends,* while Kant gives as his that each of us is

---

* Because this point has been challenged, I quote him: "Men being all the workmanship of one omnipotent and infinitely wise Maker—all the servants of one sovereign master, sent into the world by his order, and about his business—they are his property whose workmanship they are, made to last during his, not one another's pleasure; and being furnished with like

an end in himself. Locke therefore roots our dignity in God, while Kant makes us out to be gods ourselves. The two thinkers turn out to be as far apart as two thinkers can be.

Some might say the difference makes no difference; after all, Kant did reach the same conclusion as Locke, did he not? Say, rather, that he purported to. As we might have guessed from social conditions among the pagan deities, that is not the end of the story. Olympus was a world of irresistible forces and immovable objects. The gods deserved everything, but owed nothing. While expecting divine honors, they did whatever they could get away with. Solipsism produces the same result. Not everyone can have unconditional value, so beneath the high public language of equal concern and respect some become more equal than others. Because mothers are not to be means to their babies' survival, their babies become means to their mothers' control over their pregnancies. Because speakers are not to be means to their listeners' purity, their listeners become means to the speakers' pleasure in filth. Because patients are not to be means to the quiet of their doctors' consciences, their doctors become means to their patients' desire to die.

As surely as cider makes vinegar, solipsism made this evil. It would have done so *even if it were true* that being ends in ourselves keeps us from viewing others as means to ourselves. The mere idea of Not Using Others cannot produce a moral code, for only by the light of a moral code can we tell what counts as using others.

Christianity does not suffer from this vicious circle. Our faith takes its code from the One Who alone possesses unconditional value, yet Who sacrificed Himself that we may live, commanding that we

---

faculties, sharing all in one community of nature, there cannot be supposed any such subordination among us that may authorize us to destroy one another, as if we were made for one another's uses as the inferior ranks of creatures are for ours," *Second Treatise of Government*. Some have argued that Locke did not mean what he said. All I can say is that if he did not, then so much the worse for him—and for the liberal tradition.

love one another, not according to our own ideas, but as He has loved us.

ABSOLUTIONISM

The fourth moral error of political liberalism is *absolutionism*. According to this notion we cannot be blamed when we violate the moral law, either because we cannot help it, because we have no choice, or even because it *is* our choice; according to Christianity, however, we must be blamed, because we are morally responsible beings. Of course absolutionism cannot be practiced consistently, nor would it be so convenient to its practitioners if it could.

For example, a father may be absolved of child abuse because he was abused as a child himself; because of the abuse, however, the child may be absolved of murdering his father, and in this case the father is not absolved. A sodomist and a bully both may be absolved because of predisposing factors in their family or genes, but if the bully beats the sodomist, then the sodomist is absolved but not the bully. A woman may be absolved of leaving her husband because she feels trapped in the marriage, but a man is not absolved of leaving his wife for the same reason, because that would be sexist. A young man may be absolved of smashing a brick into a person's head in the excitement of a riot, but not of doing so in the excitement of a gang war, unless the motive is political, in which case he is absolved if he is a Freedom Fighter, but not if he is a Terrorist. Finally, in a reversal of vicarious atonement, the critics of absolutionism are blamed for the sins of those whom they refuse to absolve.

Nowhere does Scripture say that to know all is to forgive all. Rather it says that on the Day of Wrath, everything secret will be known and everything in darkness will come to light. Nevertheless, Christians get pulled into absolutionism by all sorts of ropes. *Ours is a God of mercy.* Yes, but He is also a God of judgment. These two qualities are united by the atoning sacrifice of Christ, of which we cannot avail ourselves unless we repent. *Christ has commanded us not to judge.* Yes, but we are not commanded not to judge acts; we are only commanded not to judge souls. We know which acts are wrong because He has told us; we do not know which souls will repent because He has not. *God loves everyone.* Yes, and that is why He wants to save us from our sins. We are not saved by good deeds, but we are certainly saved for them. God does not overlook our wrong-doing; He forgives it when we turn in faith to Christ.

In the final analysis, absolutionism is cruel, not compassionate; harsh, not lenient; malicious, not magnanimous. It speaks of mercy, but shuts out God's grace by teaching that we have no need for it. It speaks of forbearing from judgment, but its main use is to demonize class enemies. It speaks of love, but justifies evil. God forgive us for thinking there is nothing to forgive.

PERFECTIONISM

The fifth moral error of political liberalism is *perfectionism.* According to this notion human effort is adequate to cure human evil; according to Christianity our sin, like our guilt, can be erased only by the grace of God through faith in Christ. Perfectionists also think the cure can be completed in human time. Some even believe it can be arranged for whole societies at once. By contrast, the faith teaches that God must start over with each person, and that although guilt is erased immediately, the cure of sin is not complete until we are at peace with Him in heaven.

Perfectionism is rich in consequences. The war to end all wars that ushered in a century of wars, the war on poverty that spent trillions of dollars but left poverty untouched, the war on unhappiness that enriched assorted gurus while rates of suicide soared, these are but its nuts and berries. According to the faith, its final fruit is unending darkness. Yet though emptied of Hope, perfectionism is full of hopes. "Man is at last becoming aware that he alone is responsible for the realization of the world of his dreams, that he has within himself the power for its achievement"; "Humans are responsible for what we are or will become. No deity will save us; we must save ourselves"; "Man sets himself only such problems as he is able to solve." Statements like these were once considered extreme; the first and second are from the Humanist Manifestos, the third from Karl Marx. Yet today such sentiments are the boilerplate of liberal speechmaking. Remember Mr. Clinton's misquotation from Paul and Isaiah: "No eye has seen, no ear has heard, no mind has imagined what we can build," he prophesied.

Christian laxness bears some responsibility for the advent of perfectionism. For instance, today's believer does not often hear that Love is a disposition of will toward good, Faith a disposition of reason toward revealed truth, and Hope a disposition of longing toward Heaven. Once he has followed nonbelievers in using the first word for an emotion and the second for something inimical to reason, there is nothing much to stop him from using the third for complacency about the course of this present, broken world.

Other paths to perfectionism are just as well traveled. Some people even think Jesus was a perfectionist; did He not urge us to be perfect, as our Father in Heaven is perfect? But the Greek word translated "perfect," *teleioi,* means merely "complete," meaning that we are not to stop at half measures but grow up to full maturity. Thus John, who ought to have known what the Master meant, wrote in his first letter that if any man says he has no sin, he deceives himself, and the truth is not in him. Nor is perfectionism to be found in biblical prophecy. True, some Christians distort the prophecy of the millennium—the thousand-year reign of the martyrs with Christ— into the idea that worldly suffering will diminish and finally disappear through human social reform. But the text of Revelation says nothing of such things.

One sometimes hears that perfectionism is a prerequisite for pity—as though one offers a cup of cold water to a thirsty child only because he foresees an ultimate victory in the War on Thirst. On the contrary, one takes pity for the love of souls, not for the love of abstractions; moreover, one takes it because these souls are suffering, not because he expects suffering to end. Perfectionism is more likely to annihilate pity than to heighten it. All for the sake of paradise, the tyrants of our generation stacked bodies higher than Nimrod stacked bricks; yet they came no nearer heaven than he did.

UNIVERSALISM

The sixth moral error of political liberalism is *universalism*. According to this notion the human race forms a harmony whose divisions are ultimately either unreal or unimportant; according to Christianity human harmony has been shattered by sin and cannot be fully healed by any means short of conversion.

The argument that human divisions are *unreal* is usually some form of pantheism. According to the Eastern way of putting it, all is in God—the obvious consequence of which is that God includes evil. For instance, the psychiatrist Carl Jung taught that Christians are mistaken in worshiping God as Trinity. Instead they ought to worship Him as "Quaternity," the fourth Person of Godhood being Satan—a dog in the manger if ever there was one. For this some praise Jung as more "spiritual" than Freud. Most Westerners, though, prefer a formula that suppresses such unsettling conclusions: not "all is in God," but "God is in all." Thus George Fox taught that the "light of Christ" resides within each person already. By making such divisive steps as conversion unnecessary, this would seem to hold out hopes of bringing people together; actually it makes the origin and persistence of our divisions wholly mysterious.

The argument that human divisions are *unimportant* is usually some form of myopia. In one version, everyone is just like me—my class, my set, my outlook. We may all seem to want different things, but deep down we all *really* want the same thing and seek the same

God. This is the stuff of beauty pageants and Robert Fulghum books. In another version, we are all different, but that is all right because it takes all sorts. Each ingredient adds its flavor to the salad. We are the world. This is the stuff of rock telethons and multicultural curricula.

Such delusions are almost cruelly easy to explode. Did the Nazis want the same as their victims? Did they seek the same God? Did it take both sorts to make a world? Our wants are different—wealth, redemption, power, death, revenge. Our Gods are different—Yahweh, Allah, Krishna, Kali, Volk. Even our sins are different—lewdness, envy, pride, resentment, sloth. God has placed in all hearts a longing for Himself, but not every way in which we try to satisfy this longing is a search for God. A diversity of gifts has been strewn among the children of men, but not every vice or twist of the children of men is a gift. In Christ there is no slave or free, no Greek or Jew; but there *are* slave and free, and there *are* Greek and Jew.

In our time, the universalist fallacy has even given rise to a new type of professional, the "facilitator," whose bag of tricks for uncovering supposed latent unity is more and more familiar. Some of these, like active listening and decision by consensus, can be useful at times. Others, like unconditional inclusiveness, spell disaster if taken literally. What happens when they are imposed where a basis for unity is presumed that does not in fact exist? Various things; for instance the parties may stall, fly apart, or reach conspicuous agreement about points that are not at issue. At least these outcomes are straightforward. But just as often the technology of reconciliation becomes a technology of domination, more subtle than most, whose adepts simply bamboozle those who cannot talk the talk.

NEUTRALISM

The seventh moral error of political liberalism is *neutralism*. According to this notion the virtue of tolerance requires suspending judgments about good and evil; according to Christianity it requires *making* judgments about good and evil. We can break neutralism into three components. According to the Quantitative Fallacy, the meaning of tolerance is tolerating; therefore, the more you tolerate, the more tolerant you are. According to the Skeptical Fallacy, the best foundation for tolerance is to avoid having strong convictions about good and evil; therefore, the more you doubt, the more tolerant you are. According to the Apologetic Fallacy, if you cannot help having strong convictions the next best foundation for tolerance is refusing to express or act upon them; therefore, the more pusillanimous you are, the more tolerant you are.

Closely examined, each fallacy explodes itself. If you really believe that the meaning of tolerance is tolerating, then you ought to tolerate even intolerance. If you really believe that the best foundation for tolerance is to avoid having any strong convictions at all about right and wrong, then you should not have a strong conviction that intolerance is wrong. If you really believe that when you do have strong convictions you should refuse to express or act upon them, then your tolerance should be a dead letter; it should be one of the things you are pusillanimous about.

But if consistent neutralism is self-refuting, then why is it so persistent? How is it possible for it to live on in our newspapers, on the television, in the schoolroom, and even in the pulpit? There are two main reasons for its vigor. The first reason is that it *never is* practiced consistently. Rather it is used selectively as a weapon for demoralizing Christians and other opponents. For the neutralist too has strong convictions; it is just that his convictions are not the ones he says one should not act upon. Consistent neutralism would hold that if it is intolerant to express the conviction that unborn babies should not be torn from the womb, then it is also intolerant to express the conviction that they may be torn from the womb. By contrast, selective neutralism remembers itself only long enough to condemn the defenders of life.

The second reason for the vigor of neutralism is that it encourages the illusion that we can escape from moral responsibility for our beliefs and decisions. "I am innocent of this man's blood; it is your responsibility"—in these words Pilate implied that one can authorize a wrong without taking sides. "I am neither for nor against abortion; I'm for choice"—this statement is based on the same view of responsibility as Pilate's. Indeed, in trying to evade our choices we set ourselves not only against the laws of conscience but also against the laws of logic, for between two meaningful propositions X and not-X there is no middle ground; if one is true, the other is false. Even the pagans knew that.

What then is the truth about tolerance? The meaning of this virtue is not tolerating *per se,* but tolerating what ought to be tolerated. Practicing it means putting up with just those bad things that, for the sake of some greater good or of moral law, we ought to put up with. We are not practicing the virtue when we fail to put up with bad things that we ought to put up with, such as the expression of false opinions in debate; nor are we practicing it when we do put up with bad things that we ought not to put up with, such as rape. But making such distinctions requires knowing the truth about goods, bads, greater goods, and moral law. There is nothing neutral about that. It requires that we avoid not strong convictions, but false convictions; it requires not refusing to act, but acting. As Abraham Kuyper, J. B. Phillips, and C. S. Lewis have said in nearly identical words, "There is no neutral ground in the universe. Every square inch is claimed by God and counterclaimed by Satan."

COLLECTIVISM

The eighth moral error of political liberalism is *collectivism.* According to this notion the state is more important to the child than the family; according to Christianity the family is more important to the child than the state. To be sure, collectivists do not usually put their point so bluntly. A good example of hypocrisy and circumlocution is found in a court case from 1980.

In that year, the Supreme Court of the state of Washington ruled that lower courts had been right in granting fifteen-year-old Sheila Sumey's request to be taken from the Sumey home and placed in another that was more to her liking. The Sumeys were not unfit, and Sheila had not been mistreated; these points were not even at issue. Under the 1977 statute, all Sheila had to do was say that she was in "conflict" with her parents, and go on saying it after state-imposed counseling had run its course. Her "conflict" was that she disagreed with her parents' rules that she stay away from drugs and dealers, abstain from sex and alcohol, and be home every night at a reasonable hour. Mr. and Mrs. Sumey called the statute unconstitutional. The court, however, defended it as a "means for providing social services to the family and nurturing the parent-child bond." The intrusion on parental rights was "minor," it declared, because Sheila would have to petition every six months if she wanted to stay away from her parents for the rest of her minority. Although "the family structure is a fundamental institution" and "parental prerogatives are entitled to considerable legal deference," these prerogatives must yield to "fundamental rights of the child or important interests of the State."

Before collectivism, our family law was based on a philosophy that ran something like this. Growing up takes time, and until the process reaches its end children are not fully capable of deciding what is best for them. Moreover, the family is a more fundamental institution than the state, based on a closer harmony of interests among its members. From these premises we may conclude that in normal families, during the period while children are growing up, their parents may be trusted to act in their best interests. It follows that the state should not intervene except on evidence that the parents are acting abusively. In other words it should confine itself to the restraint of wickedness rather than trying to absorb the functions of the family.

The regnant political class is increasingly unhappy with this approach to growing up. Implicit in the position of the Washington court is the thought that of the two human institutions, family and state, the state is the more fundamental, and that normal families are characterized by conflict rather than harmony of interests between parents and children. From these premises the court concludes that parents should not be trusted to act in their children's best interests, and that therefore the state may intervene even when there is no evidence that parents are acting abusively. Of course parents may *become* as undependable as the state claims, but only if collectivism prevails.

Collectivism hides in a forest of reassuring bromides. "It takes a whole village to raise a child," the secular intone; "Every child is my child," the pious drowsily respond. Of all these deceptions the language of "children's rights" is the most brilliant—and also the most daring, for in no imaginable world would children be competent to exercise their "rights" themselves. The primary decision maker in the life of a child must always be, and always is, someone else: if not parents, then the state. So, although most rights limit the reach of the government, so-called children's rights increase it. They do nothing to empower children; they only empower mandarins.

I am reminded of an election-year scuffle between a father, who was also a candidate, and a social service functionary. "No government bureaucrat could love my children as I do," the father said. "That's not true," protested the functionary, "I love them just as much." "What are their names?" asked the father.

Desperate Gestures

People do wrong, and I have to do something. People are unhappy, and I have to do something. People are foolish, and I have to do something. I will absolve them. I will give them things. I will take their children. At last we come to the ninth and most mysterious moral error of political liberalism: *the fallacy of desperate gestures.*

Though it mixes with all the others, it is different from each of them, different even from perfectionism, with which it is often confused. The perfectionist acts, at least in the beginning, from a desire to relieve someone else's pain. The desperationist acts to relieve his own: the pain of pity, the pain of impotence, the pain of indignation. He is like a man who beats on a foggy television screen with a pipe wrench, not because the wrench will fix the picture but because it is handy and feels good to use.

Not long ago I sat up late listening to two friends debate. The first maintained that federal antipoverty policies were an engine of misery, which had bought off the poor with checks and coupons while undermining their families and fossilizing them in permanent dependence on the government. For a while the second denied the charge, but his denials were half-hearted and at last he conceded it. Whether the state is really doing more harm than good is not my present point; believe, if you will, that he should have held his ground. But the interesting thing is what happened next.

Having admitted that the federal antipoverty policies were do-ing harm, he defended them anyway. "What do you propose doing instead?" he demanded. "*Nothing?*" My other friend replied that he meant no such thing, and spoke of what people could do individu-ally and through the churches. Friend one was contemptuous. "Gov-ernment is unique," he said. "You cannot convince me that mere charity can take its place." "I don't want it to," said friend two. "We've already agreed that government hurts instead of helping. Besides, I'm not trying to end poverty. I don't know how. I'm just trying to help where I can reach." Friend one was unmoved. "We have to do *something*," he said, and so he went on repeating.

The two friends were at cross-purposes. The rule of the first was "Do no harm, and help where possible"; of the second, "Better to harm magnificently in the name of help, than to help but a little." Not that he would have put it that way. He was medicating his pity with symbols, and the power of the drug depends on self-deception.

Here lies the power of political liberalism: Its moral errors are fortified with opiates. We may think that reality will break through the dream by itself, but reality is not self-interpreting; the causes by which errors are eventually dissipated and replaced by other errors are hidden in God's Providence. All we can do is keep up the critique which is in the gospel, and in the meantime go on being Christians: our eyes lifted up not to the spectacular idol of political salvation, but to the Cross. Let those who will, call this doing nothing; we know better.

7

The Problem with Conservatism

Y FIRST CONSERVATIVE EXPERIENCE was in second grade, when I learned *America the Beautiful.* Verses one and two were merely baffling: I could not picture waves of grain, I could not believe that mountains were purple, and I could not form an association between liberty and pilgrim feet. But the third verse broke me like glass and made me an idolater. *O beautiful for patriot's dream, that sees beyond the years,* we warbled; *thine alabaster cities gleam, undimmed by human tears.* Somehow the song called forth in my childish heart an answering music that I had never heard in church. I seemed to hear the whine of gulls and the murmur of the sea before a white throne; I was afflicted with a sense of the Fall and a longing for the City whose light is the Glory of God. But I misidentified the City. The song sent me questing for Columbia, not the New Jerusalem. I was told to seek in the ideal futurity of my nation what cannot be made by hands.

What then is a Christian to make of conservatism? The danger, it would seem, is not in *conserving,* for anyone may have a vocation to care for precious things, but in conservative *ideology,* which sets forth a picture of these things at variance with the faith. The same is true of liberalism. From time to time Christians may find themselves in tactical alliance with conservatives, just as with liberals, over particular policies, precepts, and laws. But they cannot be in strategic alliance, because their reasons for these stands are different; they are living in a different vision. For our allies' sake as well as our own, it behooves us to remember the difference. We do not need another Social Gospel—just the gospel.

In the last chapter, I described liberalism as a bundle of acute moral errors, with political consequences that grow more and more alarming as these errors are taken closer and closer to their logical conclusions. Conservatism may be described as another such bundle. The parallel is not perfect, for American culture is balanced at the top of a liberal ridge and is only now considering the descent. Because conservative moral errors have had less time to work among the powers and principalities, we cannot always discern their political consequences. But we can anticipate their fruits by their roots. The moral errors of conservatism are just as grave as those of its liberal opponents.

A minor difficulty in setting forth these errors is the ambiguity of the term "conservatism." Conservatives come in many different kinds, and their mistakes are equally heterogeneous. I should like to stress, therefore, that not every conservative commits every one of the errors that I describe in the following pages. But there is a common theme. Each kind of conservative opposes the contemporary government-driven variety of social reformism in the name of some cherished thing which he finds that it endangers. One speaks of virtue, another of wealth, another of the peace of his home and the quiet of his street—but although these pearls are of very different luster, none wishes his to be thrown before swine. So it is that conservatives are often able to make common cause, putting all their pearls in a single casket.

CIVIL RELIGIONISM

The first moral error of political conservatism is *civil religionism.* According to this notion America is a chosen nation, and its projects are a proper focus of religious aspiration; according to Christianity America is but one nation among many, no less loved by God, but no more.

Our civil religion seems to have developed in four stages. The first stage was the Massachusetts Bay colony. Although the Puritans accepted the orthodox view of the Church as the New Israel, they also viewed the visible Church as corrupt. The Church's role of City Upon a Hill had therefore passed to themselves—to the uncorrupted remnant of the faithful, fled to North American shores. Like the Israelites, they viewed themselves as having entered into a special covenant with God to be His people. The same blessings and curses, however, were appended to their covenant as to the one at Sinai; therefore, warned Governor John Winthrop, should the settlers embrace the present world and prosecute their carnal intentions, "the Lord will surely break out in wrath against us [and] be revenged of such a perjured people."

The second stage was the colonies just before the Revolution. Increasing unity among the settlers had given rise to a *national* sense of covenant with God, but the shared experience of English harassment aroused suspicion that the covenant had been breached. Isaiah's warnings to Israel were invoked by way of explanation: "How is the faithful city become an harlot! It was full of judgment; righteousness lodged in it; but now murderers." Preachers like Samuel Langdon declared that if only the people would turn from their sins, God would remit their punishment, purge the nation of wrongdoers, restore a righteous government—and deal with the English.

The third stage was in the early and middle republic. God was still understood as the underwriter of American aspirations, but as the content of these aspirations became more and more nationalistic it also became less and less Christian. It appeared that God cared at least as much about putting down the South and taking over the West as He did about making His people holy; patriotic songwriters like Samuel Francis Smith used expressions like "freedom's holy light," but they meant democracy, not freedom from sin.

The fourth stage was the late republic. By this time American culture had become not just indifferent to Christianity, but hostile to it. Conservatives still wanted to believe that the nation was specially favored by God, but the idea of seeking His will and suffering His chastening had been completely lost. President Eisenhower remarked that what the country needed was a religious foundation, but that he did not care what it was. President Reagan applied the image of the City Upon a Hill not to the remnant of the Church in America, but to America *as such*—its mission not to bear witness to the gospel, but to spread the bits and pieces of its secular ideology.

The mistake in all these stages is confusing America with Zion. She is not the inheritor of the covenant, not the receiver of the promises, not the witness to the nations. It may well be that all nations have callings of sorts—specific purposes which God in His providence assigns them. But no nation can presume to take God under its wing. However we may love our country, dote upon her, and regret her, God can do without the United States.

INSTRUMENTALISM

The second moral error of political conservatism is *instrumentalism*. According to this notion faith should be used for the ends of the state; according to Christianity believers should certainly be good citizens, but faith should not be *used*. To be sure, the pedigree of instrumentalism is not purely conservative; it has followers on the left as well as the right. Jean-Jacques Rousseau, for instance, wanted the state to invent a civil religion to his order and *then* make use of it. Its articles would be proposed "not exactly as religious dogmas" but as "sentiments of sociability without which it is impossible to be a good citizen or a faithful subject." Most instrumentalists, however, are not so fastidious. They are willing to make a tool of whatever religion comes to hand, whether civil, traditional, or revealed. Religious conservatives who pine for the days when jurists called America "a Christian country" and recognized Christianity as "the law of the land" are deeply in error if they think such statements expressed belief; what they usually expressed was instrumentalism. In those days the religion that came to hand was Christianity (or at least its counterfeit in civil religion), and the speakers were interested primarily in how it could be used. The eminent nineteenth-century jurist Thomas Cooley admitted as much. Supreme Court Justice David Brewer, controversial author of *America a Christian Country,* was only slightly less explicit.

Viewed from this perspective, the contrast between the jurisprudence of yesterday and today is not nearly as sharp as religious conservatives make it out to be. Although language describing Christianity as the law of the land has disappeared from our cases, judges and legislators are just as interested in the social utility of the faith as they were before—and just as indifferent to its truth. Consider for example the 1984 Supreme Court case *Lynch v. Donelly,* which concerned whether a Christmastime nativity display could be financed by a municipal government. Members of the Court likened erecting a creche to adopting "In God We Trust" as the national motto and opening judicial sessions with the invocation "God save the United States and this honorable Court." By the comparison, they meant three things:

1. *These acts and declarations have nothing to do with religion.* They do not "endorse" the faith, but merely "acknowledge" it, said Justice O'Connor. Indeed they have "lost through rote repetition any significant religious content," said Justice Brennan. Otherwise, they said, they would be establishments of religion, which are forbidden.

2. *On the other hand, they are socially indispensable.* They are "uniquely" suited to serve "wholly" secular purposes (Brennan) which could not reasonably be served in any other way (O'Connor). These purposes include "solemnizing public occasions" (Brennan and O'Connor), "expressing confidence in the future and encouraging the recognition of what is worthy of appreciation in society" (O'Connor), and "inspiring commitment to meet some national challenge in a manner that simply could not be fully served if government were limited to purely nonreligious phrases" (Brennan). The last of these purposes is especially interesting—in plain language, it means getting people to do something they would refuse to do otherwise.

3. *In fact, they are a noble lie.* Obviously, if the mottoes and creches and so forth had really lost *all* their religious content, they would be completely useless for achieving any purposes whatsoever, secular or otherwise. Our rulers feel *free* to use them because they have lost religious meaning for *them;* they *work,* however, because they retain this meaning for the masses.

Moralism

The third moral error of political conservatism is *moralism.* According to this notion God's grace needs the help of the state; Christianity merely asks the state to get out of the way. We might say that while instrumentalism wants to make faith a tool of politics, moralism wants to make politics a tool of faith; on this reading, what instrumentalism is to secular conservatives, moralism is to religious conservatives. Surprisingly, though, many religious conservatives seem unable to tell the difference. Whether someone says "We need prayer in schools to make the children holy" or "We need prayer in schools to make the country strong," it sounds to them the same.

Now I am *not* going to complain that moralism "imposes" a faith on people who do not share it. In the sense at issue, even secularists impose a faith on others—they merely impose a different faith. Every law reflects some moral idea, every moral idea reflects some fundamental commitment, and every fundamental commitment is religious—it proposes a god. Everything in the universe comes to a point. For moralism, therefore, the important distinction is not between religion and secularism, but between faiths that do and faiths that do not demand the civil enforcement of all their moral precepts.

To the question "Should the civil law enforce the precepts of the faith?" the biblical answer is, "Some yes, but some no; which ones do you mean?" The New Testament contains literally hundreds of precepts. However, Christianity is not a legislative religion. While the Bible recognizes Torah as a divinely revealed code for the ruling of Israel before the coming of the Messiah, it does not include a divinely revealed code for the ruling of the Gentiles afterward. To be sure, the Bible limits the kinds of laws that Christians can *accept* from their governments, for "we must obey God rather than men" (Acts 5:29). However, it does not prescribe specific laws that they must *demand* from them.

It is not even true that *all* of God's commands limit the kinds of laws that Christians can accept. To see this, contrast two such precepts: (1) I am prohibited from deliberately shedding innocent blood; (2) I am prohibited from divorcing a faithful spouse. Both precepts are absolute in their application to *me,* but that is not the issue. If we are speaking of governmental enforcement, then we are speaking of their application to *others.* The former precept should require very little watering down in the public square, for even nonbelievers are expected to understand the wrong of murder. That is why I may be confident in condemning the legalization of abortion. But the latter precept requires a good deal of watering down in the public square, for before the coming of Christ not even believers were expected to understand the true nature of marriage. "Moses permitted you to divorce your wives because your hearts were hard," said Jesus, "but it was not this way from the beginning" (Matt. 19:8). No doubt the Pharisees were scandalized by the idea that their civil law did not reflect God's standards fully. They must have been even more offended by the suggestion that it was not intended to. Among religious conservatives this suggestion is still a scandal, but it does not come from liberals; it comes from the Master.

Christians, then, may certainly commend a law as good or condemn it as evil. They may declare it consistent or inconsistent with the faith. But not even a good law may be simply *identified* with the faith; Christians must not speak of a tax code, marriage ordinance, or welfare policy as "Christian" no matter how much, or even how rightly, they desire its enactment or preservation. *That* predicate has been preempted by the law of God. The civil law will be Christian—if it still exists at all—only when Christ Himself has returned to rule: not when a coalition of religious conservatives has got itself elected.

CAESARISM

The fourth moral error of political conservatism is *Caesarism*. According to this notion the laws of man are higher than the laws of God; according to Christianity the laws of God are higher than the laws of man. With this error we have come back to secular conservatives. The peculiar thing about the American variety of Caesarism is that the state never *says* that its laws are higher than the laws of God; in the name of equal liberty for all religious sects, it simply refuses to acknowledge *any* laws of God.

George Reynolds, a Mormon living in Utah Territory, was charged during the 1870s with the crime of bigamy. In his defense he argued that the law was an unconstitutional infringement of his free exercise of religion. Accepting his appeal, the Supreme Court disagreed. Although it said all sorts of interesting things about why free exercise of religion is good (and why polygamy is wrong—for instance because it leads to a patriarchal rather than republican principle of authority in government), the heart of the rebuttal was a simple distinction between opinions and actions. Appealing to Thomas Jefferson's idea of a "wall of separation between church and state," it held that what people believe is the business of the church, but that what they do is the business of the state. Therefore, the First Amendment does not mean that people may act as their religion requires, but only that they may think as their religion requires; free exercise of religion makes no difference whatsoever to the scope of state power over conduct.

Still favored by many conservatives, this doctrine has startling implications. It means, for instance, that in throwing Christians to the lions for refusing to worship Caesar, the Romans did nothing to infringe the free exercise of Christianity; after all, while being devoured, the martyrs were still at liberty to believe that Caesar was only a man.

A century later, in cases involving other religious groups, the Court conceded the point. Announcing its discovery that faith and conduct cannot be isolated in "logic-tight compartments," it now decreed that "only those interests of the highest order and those not otherwise served can overbalance legitimate claims to the free exercise of religion." But this was too much for judicial conservatives, and the experiment was ended in 1992. Writing for the Court in *Employment Division v. Smith (II)*, Justice Scalia appealed to the notion that the issue in free exercise cases is not whether the state's motives are "compelling," but whether they are "neutral." A law that does not expressly single out a particular sect may burden any religious practice to any degree, so long as this burden is "merely the incidental effect" of the law and not its "object." In other words, repression is fine so long as it is absentminded. Pastoral care and counselling could not be forbidden *as such* but could be forbidden as an incidental effect of regulations for the licensing of mental health practitioners; the sacrament of baptism could not be forbidden *as such* but could be forbidden as an incidental effect of regulations for bathing in public places. To be sure, since the recent action of the Court, Congress has made several attempts to reinstate the compelling-interest doctrine, lauding one bill as a "Religious Freedom Restoration Act" and another as a "Religious Liberty Protection Act." But surely this is overstatement. After all, even under the compelling-interest doctrine, claims to the free exercise of religion can be swept aside whenever the state thinks its reasons are good enough. So much we would have had without a First Amendment.

As our own times have made clear, even releasing nerve gas in public places can be an exercise of religion. Perhaps the blame for our troubles lies with the Framers, for refusing to distinguish the kinds of religion whose exercise should be free from the kinds of religion whose exercise should not. But, foolishly thinking ignorance a friend of conscience, we have followed their lead. Afraid to judge among religions, we put them all beneath our feet; pursuing the will-o'-the-wisp of equal liberty, we tumble headlong into Caesarism.

TRADITIONALISM

The fifth moral error of political conservatism is *traditionalism*. According to this notion what has been done is what should be done; Christianity, however, though it cherishes the unchanging truths of faith, insists that any merely human custom may have to be repented. "That which hath been is that which shall be; and that which hath been done is that which shall be done: and there is no new thing under the sun," writes Koheleth, "the Preacher" (Eccles. 1:9, ASV). "Behold, I will do a new thing; now shall it spring forth; shall ye not know it?" answers God (Isa. 43:19, KJV).

For the nineteenth century, of course, the best illustration of the mischiefs of traditionalism is slavery. But every evil eventually calls itself a tradition, and the latest to claim the mantle is abortion. We can best see this in the 1992 Supreme Court case *Planned Parenthood v. Casey*, which reaffirmed the supposed right to take the lives of one's unborn children. The irony is that by inventing this right in the first place, the Court had shattered tradition; no such use of lethal violence by private individuals had ever been sanctioned in common law. But *Roe v. Wade* had stood for twenty years. As far as the Court is concerned, that makes it a new tradition—and as such, unassailable. Amazingly, the Court upheld *Roe* even while admitting that it might have been decided incorrectly, and despite the brevity of the tradition, the reasoning at this point is purely traditionalist. "We are satisfied," declared Justices Kennedy, O'Connor, and Souter, "that the immediate question is not the soundness of *Roe*'s resolution of the issue, but the precedential force that must be accorded the ruling." And their opinion carried the day. Just how does an unsound precedent have force? The answer, say the justices, is that "for two decades of economic and social developments, people have organized their intimate relationships and made choices that define their views of themselves and their places in society in reliance on the availability of abortion in the event that contraception should fail. . . . An entire generation has come of age free to assume Roe's concept of liberty." To put the idea more simply, sex has been separated from responsibility for resulting children for so long that to change the rules on people now would be unfair. Never mind whether what was done was right; what matters is that it was done.

Moral errors gain their plausibility from the truths that they distort. It is certainly true that precedents, traditions, and customs should not be needlessly disturbed; the gain in goodness from a particular change must always be balanced against the harm of change *as such*. But this truth applies to the choice between a good law and a still better one, not to the choice between a good law and an evil one. The question to ask about moral evil is not whether we have got used to it, but whether it can be stopped.

NEUTRALISM

The sixth moral error of political conservatism is *neutralism*. This may come as a surprise, because we learned in the previous chapter that neutralism also comes in a liberal variety. Whereas the liberal sort of neutralist exclaims, "Let a thousand flowers bloom," the conservative sort cries merely, "Leave me alone." In essence, conservative neutralism is the notion that because everyone ought to mind his own business, moral and religious judgments should be avoided. By contrast, while agreeing that one ought to mind his own business—St. Paul warns three times against busybodies—Christianity holds that moral and religious judgments can never be avoided. They must be straight and true before people can even agree as to what their business is.

Not everyone reaches neutralism by the same route, but the conservative thinker Michael Oakeshott follows a well-worn path in deriving it from traditionalism. Conservatives, he says, seek activities whose enjoyment springs "not from the success of the enterprise, but from the familiarity of the engagement." What makes this disposition intelligible in politics is "the observation of our current manner of living" together with the belief that laws are "instruments enabling people to pursue activities of their own choice with minimum frustration." But to say this is to reject the view that laws are "plans for imposing substantive activities"; therefore, he holds, conservatism has "nothing to do" with morals or religion.

Of course the conclusion does not follow, and if it were really true then conservatives could make no decisions at all. Rather than being indifferent to questions of good and evil, Oakeshott himself maintains the good of minimizing frustration, and rather than holding no opinion about religion, he holds the opinion that it is better to be ignorant of truth than to be pestered about it. For example he says that people of conservative disposition "might even be prepared to suffer a legally established ecclesiastical order," but "it would not be because they believed it to represent some unassailable religious truth, but merely because it restrained the indecent competition of sects and (as Hume said) moderated 'the plague of a too diligent clergy.'" The difficulty is plain: If not by his own moral and religious standards, then how does Oakeshott know that competition is indecent and diligence a plague? Why not condemn complacency and sloth instead?

Not even rules *designed* to tell what counts as pestering can work in a neutral way. Always we must add others to make them work—and what we add makes a difference to the outcome. Christianity recognizes this. For example, consider the principles of Subsidiarity and Sphere Sovereignty. Each targets the problem of knowing where the business of one party ends and the business of another begins. Subsidiarity, a precept prominent in Catholic social thought, holds that greater and higher social institutions like the state exist just to *help* lesser and subordinate ones like the family. Therefore, to destroy the lesser institutions, absorb them, or take away their proper functions is "gravely wrong" and a "disturbance of right order." Sphere subsidiarity is more prominent in Protestant social thought. Ordering social institutions horizontally instead of vertically, it says that each has its own domain, its own authority, and its own ruling norm, for instance love in the case of the family and public justice in the case of the state. Therefore, each should be protected from interference by the others.

Both rules are meant to deal with meddling, but applying either one requires a vast amount of other knowledge which one must get from somewhere else—just what the neutralist would like to think unnecessary. To test my college students I used to ask, "To which institution would a subsidiarist give the task of instructing children in sexual mores—state or family?" Almost all replied, "The state." Families need *help*, they argued, because they do a poor job in this area: they rarely teach children about contraception, sexual preferences, or the many other things which young moderns need to know.

I was astonished. Couldn't my students tell the difference between helping the family and absorbing its functions? On reflection their answer was not astonishing at all. They shared neither Christian presuppositions about what sex is for nor Christian presuppositions about how a family works; why then should they have reached Christian conclusions in applying Christian social principles?

There is nothing exceptional about the principles of Subsidiarity and Sphere Sovereignty; *no* definition of meddling or intrusion can work in a neutral way. Particular moral and religious understandings are always presupposed, and changing them changes the way our definitions work. It follows that forbidding moral judgments will not keep busybodies out of other people's hair. Somehow they must learn the meanings of "other," "people's," and "hair."

MAMMONISM

The seventh moral error of political conservatism is *mammonism.* According to this notion wealth is the object of commonwealth, and its continual increase even better; according to Christianity wealth is a snare, and its continual increase even worse. Mammonism is what the Big Tent that some political analysts urge for the Republican Party is all about: ditch the social issues, but keep that capital gains tax reduction. To hold onto your liberty you have to hold onto your money.

Christians, of course, are not the only ones to have criticized mammonism. Warnings against the love of wealth were a staple even of ancient pagan conservatism. The idea was that virtue makes republics prosper, but prosperity leads to love of wealth, love of wealth leads to loss of virtue, and loss of virtue makes republics fall. Thus if you want your republic to endure, you will do well to seek a site unfavorable to great prosperity—not too warm, not too fertile, not too close to the trading routes. That our secular conservatives disagree with their ancient counterparts will strike no one as a new idea. Odder is the ease with which modern Christians make their peace with mammonism.

One of the crasser examples is found in the late-nineteenth-century Baptist preacher Russell Conwell, who maintained that to make money is the same thing as to preach the Christian gospel. However that may be, to preach his own gospel was certainly the same thing as to make money. So eager were people to hear his oft-repeated *Acres of Diamonds* speech that he is said to have earned, over a period of years, perhaps six million dollars from speakers' fees alone. Though peanuts by the standards of modern televangelists, at the time that was real money. An inventory of Conwell's more astonishing claims would include at least the following: (1) It is your Christian duty to get rich, and ownership of possessions makes you a better person; (2) The overwhelming majority of rich people are morally upright, and that is exactly why they are rich; (3) It is wrong to be poor, and God does not approve of poor people. That Jesus explicitly contradicts each of these claims (Matt. 6:19-21, Matt. 19:23-24, Luke 6:20) leaves Conwell cold.

A more temperate but still objectionable form of mammonism is found in *Toward the Future,* a "lay letter" published in 1984 by a committee of prominent Catholic conservatives. Jesus tells the story of a master who entrusts his servants with his money while he travels to a distant place to receive a kingship. Upon his return, he finds that one servant has buried his share while the other two have made investments. The timid servant he scolds and dismisses, but the bold ones he praises and rewards with yet greater responsibilities. Traditionally, the Church has understood this parable to mean that just as a king in this world expects his agents to take risks, not burying his money but investing it to earn a return, so God expects his people to take risks, not burying their gifts but using them to build up the Kingdom of Heaven. By contrast, the lay letter understands it to mean simply that God expects his people to invest their money to earn a return. "Preserving capital is not enough," the authors teach. "It must be made to grow." The use of gifts for the sake of the Kingdom becomes the growth of wealth for its own sake.

To be sure, the lay letter's defense of enterprise is not altogether wrong. Material things are not intrinsically evil, it is not a sin to engage in honest business, and, despite its dubious motivational underpinnings, the capitalist type of economy may well be superior to the alternatives. Indeed the cooperative sort of socialism seems to ignore the circumstance of the Fall, and the compulsory sort cannot even be established without the sin of theft. In a fallen world, much can also be said for the "invisible hand" of the market, by which independent individuals, even though selfish, bring about a social good which was no part of their intention. But even Adam Smith recognizes that the invisible hand does not work unless laborers and businessmen submit themselves to the restraints of justice, and that an interest in wealth alone will not induce them to do so. After all, if winning is all that matters, why keep the competition going at all? Why not use one's wealth to wring special privileges from the government and so become more wealthy still? Capitalism depends on a moral spirit which it cannot supply and may even weaken; it is, in the most exact of senses, a *parasite* on the faith. But a Christian parasite is not by that fact Christian.

MERITISM

The eighth moral error of political conservatism is *meritism*. According to this notion I should do unto others as they deserve. With the addition of mammonism, matters become even simpler, for then those who need help are by definition undeserving, while those in a position to help are by definition deserving. That meritism is not a Christian doctrine comes as a surprise to many people. Large numbers think the meritist motto "God helps those who help themselves" is a quotation from the Bible. What the New Testament actually teaches is that in what we need most, we are helpless; the grace of

God is an undeserved gift. According to Christianity I should do unto others not as they deserve, but as they need.

Aristotle taught that vices tend to come in pairs, because one can miss a mark either by way of excess or by way of deficiency—by going too far or by failing to go far enough. That is certainly the case here, for the conservative mistake of meritism stands opposite to the liberal mistake of propitiationism—doing unto others as they *want*. In fact the commonest way to fall into either mistake is by sheer recoil from the other. The reason is easy to see: we tend to think of justice and mercy as antithetical, so that to practice either, I must slight the other. By this line of reasoning the conservative emphasis on desert is a preference for justice, while the liberal emphasis on desire is a preference for mercy. By contrast, in the Christian account of things justice and mercy are *corollaries* that must be united. They are united in the Atonement because God neither waived the just penalty for our sins nor inflicted it on us, but took it upon Himself. This staggering gift also teaches what the unity of justice and mercy requires: sacrifice. If to *us* justice and mercy seem irreconcilable, the reason is probably that we are loath to pay the price of their reconciliation; we are afraid of sacrifice and shrink from the way of the Cross.

What does the contrast between meritism and charity look like in ordinary human relationships? Consider the governmental policy of paying women cash prizes for bearing children out of wedlock. Liberals want to continue the policy because they cannot tell need from desire. Meritists propose ending it because the subsidies are undeserved. Although a Christian may accept the cutoff, he cannot accept it for the reason given. All of us at all times need and receive many things that we do not deserve. The problem with the subsidies is that they are *not* what is needed. They so completely split behavior from its natural consequences that they infantilize their supposed beneficiaries; to infantilize them is to debase them, and no one needs to be debased.

Very well, says the meritist to the Christian, but we both support a cutoff. The rationales differ, but so what? That makes no difference in practice, does it? But it does. After achieving the cutoff, the meritist thinks his work is done, but the Christian thinks his work has only begun. He must now find another way to offer help; and he had better be prepared to pay the price. For a portrait of that price, think not of a bureaucrat; think of Mother Teresa.

THE RIGHT REFERENCE GROUP

We have considered what Christians are to make of political conservatism. It might also be asked what political conservatives are to make of Christians. I am afraid that the more faithful we are to our identity in Christ, the less reliable they will find us even as occasional allies; and we must be honest with them. Michael Novak wrote in his 1969 book *A Theology for Radical Politics* that because God is the source of all truth and good, whatever is true and good is *ipso facto* Christian. At that time finding truth and goodness on the left, he therefore baptized the left. Like many Christians of the time, what he forgot was that in order to identify the true and the good, one must have a standard. "Every explanation of the meaning of human existence," said Reinhold Niebuhr, "must avail itself of some principle of explanation which cannot be explained. Every estimate of values involves some criterion of value which cannot be arrived at empirically." By the time he wrote *Confessions of a Catholic,* fourteen years later, Novak had arrived at the same insight. As he explained, his former self had erred in taking his principle of explanation and criterion of value from a worldly faction instead of the community of faith. The "reference group" of Christian activists like himself had somehow become "others on the left"; it should have been others in the Lord.

To repeat the error in reverse would be a shame, for the reference group of Christians can no more be others on the right than others on the left. Citizenship is an obligation of the faith; therefore the Christian will not abstain from the politics of the nation-state. But his primary mode of politics must always be *witness*. It is a good and necessary thing to change the welfare laws, but better yet to go out and feed the poor. It is a good and necessary thing to ban abortion, but better yet to sustain young women and their babies by taking them into the fellowship of faith. This is the way that the kingdom of God is built. It is not by the world that the world is moved; may we not be moved by it either.

8

Why We Kill the Weak

I F WE MAY KILL, we may do anything—and historians will write that by the last decade of the twentieth century, great numbers of men and women in the most pampered society on the earth had come to think it normal and desirable that their sick, their weak, and their helpless should be killed. When they were a poor country, they had not so thought; now in the day of their power and prosperity, they changed their minds. Babies asleep in the dim of the womb were awakened by knife-edged cannulas that sucked and tore at their soft young limbs; white-haloed grandmothers with wandering minds were herded by white-smocked shepherds into the cold dark waters of death. Many physicians came to think of suicide as though it were a medicine.

How is it even possible to think such thoughts? How can so many of our neighbors have been persuaded of their truth? How can a mind entertain the goodness of evil for as much as a moment without curling up and returning to dust? The paradox is as sharp as a broken bone, for it is not as though the people of our place and time have ceased thinking of what is right and good. That is not even a possibility for human minds. No, our neighbors tell themselves that they are *doing* the right and good.

Therein lies the mystery—and the culmination of the mysteries, mendacities, and confusions this book has discussed. Our time will be an emblem for future times of the capture of a culture by sin. At least it will be an emblem for them if they have repented.

There is a rule for probing such mysteries. We may call it the Asymmetry Principle, for it holds that one can only understand the bad from the good, not the good from the bad. Do we want to know how it is possible to be foul? Then we have to know how it is possible to be fair. Have we need to fathom the spreading desire to kill all those who have the greatest claim on our protection? Then we must fathom the good impulses from whose pollution this bad one comes.

In Augustine's day, the Manichaeans proposed a different principle. In their view, evil did not require any special explanation because it was one of the primordial realities. There are good things like light, health, and virtue, and there are bad ones like darkness, disease, and sin. Both have existed from the beginning; a good deity created all the former, and a bad deity created all the latter. That's all.

Although the Manichaean view seems simpler, it cannot be true. Everything bad is just a good thing spoiled. I can block the light in order to cast shadow pictures on the wall, but I cannot block the dark in order to cast bright ones. I can ruin a man's health to make him sick, but I cannot ruin his sickness to make him well. The veriest devil must possess the goods of existence, intelligence, power, and will; they become evil only through their disordered condition. Augustine taught us this.

What then are those goods whose pollution produces the wish to destroy the weak? Perhaps the most important are pity, prudence, amenity, honor, remorse, love, and the sense of justice. Let us consider how each in turn is spoiled.

Spoiled Pity

In his ruminations on the original condition of mankind, Jean-Jacques Rousseau called pity an innate repugnance to see one's fellow suffer. Even animals have it, he said, for cattle low upon entering a slaughterhouse and a horse does not willingly pass near a corpse. The idea seems to be that the sight of pain makes me feel pain myself, and I do not like it. My pity is ultimately self-regarding.

This definition rather misses the point. True pity is a heartfelt sorrow for the suffering of another, seen or not, moving us to render what aid we can. True, there may be something self-regarding in pity—by rendering aid, I do alleviate the pain I feel as a witness—but my focus is on the pain of the other. By contrast, in Rousseauan "pity" the self-regarding element has taken over. Yes, rendering aid to the other would alleviate my pain; but if there is an easier way to escape the terrible spectacle, then from a Rousseauan point of view, so much the better. I can run away; I can turn my back; I can close my eyes. Perhaps that is why Rousseau left all his own children at orphanages.

But though Rousseau's definition fails dismally for true pity, for spoiled pity it works perfectly well. The purpose of pity is to prime the pump of loving-kindness, but when we refuse to use it in that way the impulse is merely displaced. While in true pity we move closer to the sufferer, in degraded pity we move farther. While in true pity we try to change the painful sight, in degraded pity we merely try to make it go away. And there are lots of ways to do that.

Then again maybe there are not. In a society like ours, with no more frontier and hardly enough room to turn around, killing the sufferer may well be the cheapest and easiest way of making the painful sight go away. As someone said in the case of George DeLury, imprisoned for poisoning and suffocating his sick wife, I may say I am putting her out of her misery, but I am really putting her out of mine.

SPOILED PRUDENCE

Some things and persons must be entrusted to my care, and others to yours. Wiser than Marx, even Plato proposed communism only with tongue in cheek; he laughed about it, said it could never be achieved by human means, and admitted that even if it could be, it would never last. Not caring even for the joke, Aristotle taught that when things are held in common they are not well cared for. We need homes, not warrens, families, not orphanages, and belongings, not tribal hoards. In the eyes of God my young children, my ancient parents, and my personal affairs are not really mine; I have been made merely a caretaker for them. But that standard is too high for the law, which must accommodate itself to the fact of sin—including the sin of busybodiness. It may be fashionable to say that it takes a whole village to raise a child—and it is certainly true that parents need to support each other—but a wiser proverb is that with the whole village kibitzing, I cannot properly take care of anyone or anything.

Prudence, then, is good judgment and conscientious care for the things and the persons entrusted to me. We may call it the insight and impulse of responsible stewardship.

Perhaps it is not hard to see how the legal standard is confused with the moral norm—how stewardship decays into ownership. I come to think that my life, my affairs, and my relatives *really are* mine, mine in the ultimate sense, and that I may do with them as I please. After this, just one little step takes me to the sheer urge to control. The urge is bad, but we can never understand it if we think of it as *simply* bad. Consider, for example, how hard it is to shame people who insist on control. They do not merely resist; they become indignant, *morally* indignant, as though someone were interfering with their virtue. Why is this? Because the bad impulse to be in control is parasitic on the good impulse to exercise responsible stewardship—an impulse which has its own proper place in the order of things and its own proper claim on the conscience.

Spoiled prudence, then, manifests itself in the notion that I have the *right* to protect my life from the distractions of your suffering and dependence, and the *right* to manipulate you in the manner most convenient to me. These notions make strange bedfellows: the modern feminist agrees with the ancient Roman father that children are merely an extension of one's body, and the Dutch agree with the Eskimos that the old have a duty to get out of the way. But we should not be surprised. If the potentiality for prudence is universal, then the potentiality for its corruption must be universal as well.

Spoiled Amenity

Amenity, or complaisance, is the impulse every person has to accommodate himself to all the rest. Like every moral impulse it carries sanctions: in this case, fear of rejection and desire to belong. But as with every moral impulse, the sanctions are only training wheels, preparing us for obedience to a deeper moral principle written on the heart. A mature person accommodates himself to others not just from fear of rejection and desire to belong, but from concern for their legitimate interests.

The problem, of course, is that in many of us the impulse never does mature. We continue to rely on the training wheels and never learn to ride. Unfortunately, this makes a difference. Mature amenity draws a boundary; precisely because I care about the legitimate interests of others, my willingness to accommodate has a limit. At just the point where going along would not be good for all, I call a halt. Stunted amenity cannot make such distinctions. It cannot stop accommodating; it does not know how. I give Grandma lethal drugs to accommodate my relatives; to accommodate me, Grandma asks for lethal drugs. A girl has an abortion to accommodate her boyfriend; to accommodate his girlfriend, the boy goes along. We know these things are wrong, but for fear of being on the outs with others we do them anyway. In the extreme case, we accommodate each other to death.

Of course people suffer remorse when they commit these terrible deeds. For present purposes, the more interesting fact is that they also tend to suffer remorse when they refuse to commit them. When they hold out, when they say no, when they resist the clamor of voices telling them what to do, they feel not only afraid, but *in the wrong.* This shows that, like prudence, the urge to accommodate is not *simply* self-regard even when it is spoiled and self-regarding. It draws strength from the very sense of obligation that it corrupts. Conscience always does the best it can; when driven from its proper course, it finds another and flows on.

SPOILED HONOR

To honor someone is to show him the reverence due to him as a fellow image of God, distinct from myself, sent into the world for the Creator's pleasure and not my own. The impulse to honor others is the best vaccine against the urge to control them, but it suffers from corruptions of its own.

In one case within my experience, a woman tried to honor her husband by sparing him what she thought would be a dreadful ordeal. "If I ever become a burden to you," she said, "I want you to pull the plug." Although this was not to his liking at all, he tried to honor her in turn by giving her his promise. Before considering the outcome, let us consider what was wrong with each deed.

What spoiled the woman's attempt to honor her husband was that she did not treat him as a moral being. Had he become helpless she would have borne any burden to care for him; she demeaned him by thinking he needed to be spared bearing burdens to care for her. What she thought honoring him violated the Golden Rule, for she would not allow him to do for her what she rightly would have wanted to do had she been in his place.

What spoiled the husband's attempt to honor his wife was that he made her an illicit promise. He forgot that it is impossible to reverence the image of God in another by complying with what soils that image. Had *he* expressed an immoral wish, he would have wanted her to challenge him; yet when she expressed an immoral wish, he would not challenge her. So he violated the Golden Rule too.

The outcome? She did, in time, become sick and dependent, and she wanted him, for his sake, to keep his promise. In an unseemly rush, not wanting to but believing he had to, he did. She died, he grieved most terribly—and he found himself unable to stop. The trauma of her death was overwhelmed by the trauma of his killing her. To the end of his own life, many years later, remorse made each day like the day that her heart had stopped. With the thought of sparing him a burden that he could have borne, she had thrust on him another burden that he could not. Complying with her wish, he had made that burden his own. Trapped by spoiled honor on every side, he did not even know how to repent.

Spoiled Remorse

Guilt is an objective reality—the condition of being in violation of moral law. By contrast, remorse is a subjective reality—the *feeling* of being in violation of moral law. What is the purpose of the feeling? Obviously, to prod us into recognition of the condition so that we can repent and throw ourselves upon the mercy of God.

It may seem strange that remorse could ever get us into trouble instead of out of it. On the contrary, nothing is more common. Like every moral impulse, remorse can be displaced. It can refuse the relief of repentance and seek alleviation in another way instead. In the short term, remorse can even be palliated by further wrongdoing. The first murder in history was undertaken from spoiled remorse. Cain's sacrifice had been unacceptable to God; he killed his righteous brother to get rid of the reminder of his shame.

Women sometimes even have abortions because of remorse over previous abortions. There was the woman who was afraid God would "do something" to the new baby to punish her for killing the other, so she beat Him to the punch. And there was the woman of chapter two, who had her first abortion out of anger because her husband had been unfaithful to her, and her second because "I wanted to be able to hate myself more for what I did to the first baby." In much the same way that some people use one credit card to pay off another, she was trying to abate her present remorse by increasing her burden of future remorse.

We may be sure that spoiled remorse is just as great a motive for killing the sick and the old. For years, perhaps, I have neglected my aging father. Now, when he is weak and dependent, the burden of my conscience has become intolerable. I cannot bear the reproach of his watery eyes; I would rather endure the blows of his fists than the sight of his withered, lumpy hands. To avoid him I visit him less and less. One day he requires hospitalization and cannot feed himself. He is not dying, he is not unconscious, he is not even in great discomfort; nevertheless I tell his caretakers to withdraw his food and water. It is easier to face them than to face him, for he is the sole surviving witness to the slights of his ungrateful son. Besides, I tell myself, I no longer deserve a father. When his body is buried, perhaps my guilt will be buried as well.

SPOILED LOVE

Love is a perfect determination of the will to further the true good of another person. As such, it can miss the mark in either of two different ways. If the will is unsteady, then we call the love weak; if the understanding is bent, then we call the love spoiled. The faults of weak love are faults of omission, in that I fail to care sufficiently for the one who needs my mercy. But the faults of spoiled love are faults of commission, in that I may actually do him harm.

Although the modes of spoiled love are infinite in number, it may suffice to mention two. In one mode, what stunts my charity is a failure to understand the involvement of each human being in all the others. Many of us have known parents who have abortions for the sake of a child already born. They actually suppose that Johnny is an island, entire to himself; that it will be better for him if Sally is cut in pieces before her birth, because with one less child their home will be quieter and their finances more secure. In this frame of mind, Grandma too seems a threat to the younger members of the family. Isn't she just a useless eater? Up there in her nursing home she merely consumes while giving nothing back. Of course I do not mind spending time and money on her *myself*—after all, she *is* my mother—but why must my *child* do with less?

It is difficult to explain the wrong of abortion to someone who thinks it is better for Johnny to have a trip to Disney World than a baby sister, difficult to explain the wrong of euthanasia to one who thinks he will be more blessed learning to take than learning to sacrifice for a lady who needs his mercy.

In the other mode of spoiled love, what stunts my charity is a failure to understand the good of affliction. "Truly . . . affliction is a treasure," says John Donne, "and scarce any man hath enough of it." Of course, no one should seek affliction or gratuitously impose it on another, but is there a soul alive who has not learned more from his hard times than his good? How dare we then imagine that our dear ones are like animals, who, when they suffer, have nothing to learn from it, and are fit only to be "put out of their misery"? What arrogance is it that denies to the sick at the last that teacher to which each of us is most indebted?

But this is an even harder lesson than the last one. That for fallen natures physical suffering may sometimes accomplish moral good, is a fact of everyday experience, but for people who do not even believe in spanking it may be hard to teach.

THE SPOILED SENSE OF JUSTICE

The sense of justice is the desire to see that each is given his due— that the good are rewarded and the bad are punished. It is not hard to see how a spoiled sense of justice can make me feel justified in mistreating someone weak who I think has hurt me in the past.

Perhaps I nurse a grievance against my parents for wrongs done to me when they were large and strong and I was small and weak; now the tables are turned and I finally have the chance to pay them out. Perhaps they did not really wrong me but I think they did. Beyond a certain point, indulgence merely generates a feeling of entitlement. Eventually the feeling becomes so great that nothing can satisfy it. My generation has been more indulged, and consequently has a stronger sense of grievance, than any other in history. Of course resentment is an unpleasant feeling, but if I can convert it into moral indignation I feel much better.

Even more alarming is the tendency of the guilty conscience to call spoiled justice to its aid by *inventing* grievances. Cause and effect here trade places: we think of resentment coming first and mistreatment coming after, but it is often the other way around. People almost always resent the people they have treated worst, as a defense against the shame of having treated them so poorly in the first place. Unfortunately, such effects take on a life of their own and become real causes after all. Having invented a grievance to justify my neglect, I may now act in malice at the prompting of the grievance. I may resent my father for no reason other than that I have mistreated him; nevertheless, having invented a fictitious reason for mistreating him, I now feel justified in wanting him to die.

Not that I am likely to be so honest with myself about my thoughts. I may not admit my resentment at all, because we do not call it "just" to kick a man when he is down. But my secret sense of grievance will always be a finger on the scale of my benevolence, biasing me toward what anyone but myself would recognize as spite.

THE ROAD TO HELL

There is a fallacy in our judgments about these things; it results from a distinction we ought not to make. Some wrongdoing, we say, should be treated with lenity because it is committed with good motives. Other wrongdoing, we say, should be treated harshly because it is committed with bad ones. She killed her sick father out of desire for his inheritance, so she should be judged; he killed his sick mother out of sympathy for her pain, so he should be pardoned. She had an abortion because her exams were coming up, so she should be condemned; he supported the abortion out of respect for her decision, so he should be excused.

Distinguishing among motives is often no more than a way to let ourselves off the hook while keeping the others on it. After all, we know our own motives much better than we can ever know theirs; therefore we know the good in our motives much better than the good in theirs. We are always in a better position to plead extenuating circumstances in *our* case.

But that is not the main problem with pardoning wrongs that are done from good motives. The main problem is that *all* wrongs are done from good motives. As we said at the beginning, there is no such thing as pure or perfect evil; every bad thing is a good thing spoiled. Without good motives to corrupt, there could be no wrongdoing at all. Did George DeLury kill his wife because he hated the sight of her suffering? Then the motive was spoiled pity. Did he do it to stay in control? Then it was spoiled prudence. To go along with her wishes? Spoiled amenity. To keep a promise? Spoiled honor. To bury his shame, to put her out of her misery, to pay her back for hurting him? Spoiled remorse, spoiled love, spoiled sense of justice. That the raw material of his intention was *good* was the condition of his having an intention at all. But that he *ruined* that good material through a free exercise of his will was what made the intention evil.

To understand all wrong is not to excuse all wrong; rather, to understand it is to know why it is wrong. Yet achieving such understanding is far from useless. From the throne of mercy there may yet be mercy for a merciless generation, but not before we know what we have done. We had best get started, for we have done a great deal.

9

The Fallen City
(reprise and charge)

EVERY DAY the position of Western Christians seems more and more like the position of the early Christians in pagan Rome. Really it never ceased to be like that, for although for some time in some countries the rulers have made free with the name of Christ, and although for some time in some countries the bread of the law has been leavened by the word of God, the world has never become the city of God; it remains for the most part the city of Man against God. Consider our own dear country: a nation conspicuous for its Christian origins, whose Congress once proclaimed days of prayer and fasting, and whose very coinage defies the gods of wealth by declaring trust in God. Yet more and more, one has the feeling of wandering in a phantasmagorical dream-house in which nothing is as it seems. Solid objects cannot be trusted to be solid; empty space cannot be trusted to be empty. Hands pass through walls, yet bodies cannot pass through an open door. The floor quakes, though it ought to be as steady as rock; should one step on the wrong tile, a trap-door opens and you slide down a chute into Somewhere Else. In some of our cities there are more abortions than live births. A guardian of the laws who lies under oath is held to be doing a "good job."

A man sues his girlfriend for getting pregnant, saying she "intentionally acquired and misused" his semen. Scientists contemplate mixing the genomes of humans and chimpanzees. Network television producers invite a serial medical killer to commit his next homicide on the air.

Almost all citizens profess to be shocked. Most are lying.

The analogy with the pagans may seem too strong, because Western Christians are no longer (or not yet) tortured and killed, as they are to the tune of three hundred thousand annually in the rest of the world. Yes, but in another way the analogy is not strong enough. Neo-pagans do not have the excuse of real pagans, that they have not heard. Rather, they have heard, and rejected. Rejection lays a greater burden on the conscience and presses a greater distorting force against the mind. On the last day, it may go heavier for the average smirking postmodernist than for Caligula, whose madness was in part, perhaps, involuntary. To make oneself out to be Zeus as he did is pretty small potatoes anyway, compared with what our intellectuals claim for themselves. Not even Zeus supposed that he was a "creator of his own values."

So long as he remains in this world, every Christian has two responsibilities. The first is to put on the mind of Christ; the second is to carry that mind into the post-Christian public square—into whatever is public, whether that should mean media, marketplace, or profession, or include university, association, or Congress.

Various vanities hinder putting on the mind of Christ. One is *quietism,* thinking that Christ need not make a difference in the public square just because the public square is not the Church. Another, particularly strong among scholars, is *positivism,* thinking that although Christ should make a difference to what we do in the public square, he should make no difference to how we study it because we should "suspend" our world views and "let the facts speak for themselves." A third is *accommodationism,* imagining that we have put on the mind of Christ already just because we have absorbed one of the secular ideologies and called it Christian. The answer to quietism is to affirm the difference between the Church and the public square, but point out that Christ is interested in both. The answer to positivism is to affirm the need for objectivity, but point out that facts never speak for themselves; one must have a certain view of the created world to believe that there are facts at all. And I have been answering accommodationism throughout this book.

Most of those who have got this far will understand all of this already. The greater difficulty is not putting on the mind of Christ *about* the public square but carrying it outdoors *into* the public square.

WITNESS

Every Christian should be ready to bear public witness, of course, but it is a systematic necessity for two groups of Christians in particular. In the first group are the *evangelists,* called to bear public witness to the "special" or "saving" grace by which God redeems those who turn to Christ in faith. In the second group are the *sustainers,* called to bear public witness to the "common" or "preserving" grace by which he keeps the unredeemed world from becoming even worse than it is already. We depend on common grace, not saving grace, when we try to leaven the civil law that we share with our unbelieving neighbors: for instance in seeking agreement with them that life in the womb should not be destroyed, that sodomy should not be granted legal equivalence with marriage, or that sick people should be cared for and comforted instead of starved or pressured into suicide. Only by common grace have we common ground; it does not "happen by itself."

From Scripture and tradition, we know a great deal about the vocation to evangelize, but not much about the vocation to sustain; a great deal about the grace that saves, but not much about the grace that preserves; a great deal about shedding light, but not much about strewing salt. That is too bad, because it is the sustainers, not the evangelists, for whom a book like this is written, and whom it hopes to encourage. But the data are not nearly so sparse as they seem. Surprisingly, the Bible does not make the claim that God's basic moral requirements are revealed nowhere else but in itself. In fact it tells of at least five other ways in which God, by his common or preserving grace, has made them known. Because of this universal instruction, this general moral revelation, no human being can honestly claim to be altogether ignorant of the natural law. It is not something that flows *from* human nature, as though God had nothing to do with it; it is something impressed *upon* human nature, and God has everything to do with it. Even those who have never heard of the natural law have felt it pressing upon their inward parts.

First is the witness of conscience, on which so much of this book has dwelt. In Romans 2, Paul says that even the pagans know God's basic moral law because it is "written on their hearts, their consciences also bearing witness." Their sins come not from genuine moral ignorance but from stubbornness or denial, for they "hold the truth [down] in unrighteousness" (Rom. 1:18, KJV)—they "suppress it by their wickedness" (NIV). How much more true of modern people, whose sense of general revelation is sharpened even by the special revelation which they also reject.

Second is the witness of Godward longing. Acts 17 records that the Athenians built an altar to a god they could not name. At some level they knew their idols could never save; moreover they had an intuition of a Holy One who could, a god "in whom we live and breathe and have our being" and who is somehow our Father. This is a moral intuition, insofar as it tells us that we were made not for ourselves, but for Him.

Third is the witness of His handiwork. Paul and David say creation cries out about its eternal, glorious, powerful, and merciful Creator. (Ps. 19:1-6, Ps. 104, Acts 14:17, Rom. 1:20) Not only do the heavens proclaim the glory of God, but so do our very forms. "For you created my inmost being," says David; "you knit me together in my mother's womb. I praise you because I am fearfully and wonderfully made" (Ps. 139:13-14a). Not even the abortionist can wholly shut out the knowledge of what he has taken to pieces; it shudders down the ventricles of scruple and trembles through the arteries of surmise. "The sensations of dismemberment flow through the forceps like an electric current," wrote abortionist Warren Hern. "Some part of our cultural and perhaps even biological heritage recoils." Yes, he could count himself a king of infinite space, were it not for bad dreams.

Fourth is the witness of the harvest. As Scripture repeatedly assures, every sin is linked with consequences; whatever we sow, we reap (Prov. 1:31, Jer. 17:10, Hos. 10:12, Gal. 6:7). People may pretend ignorance of these consequences, as our people still pretend ignorance of the harvest of the sexual revolution. Yet there is a difference between playing dumb and being dumb.

Fifth is the witness of our design. God makes some of His intentions plain just through the way He made us—He stamps them on the "blueprint," the plan of our physical and emotional design. Why else would Paul call homosexual intercourse "against nature"? (Rom. 1:26-27). In the same way, no one celebrates a D&C, but everyone celebrates a birth. I observed to a homosexual activist with whom I was debating that our bodies have a language of their own, that we say things to each other by what we do with them. What does it *mean* then, I asked him, when a man puts the part of himself which represents the generation of life into the cavity of decay and expulsion? Seeing the answer all too well, he refused to reply. Permit me to spell it out. It means "Life, be swallowed up by death."

So it is that unconverted Gentiles, who have neither waited at the foot of Sinai nor sat at the feet of Jesus, are still accountable to God. Do we grasp the implication? Most defenses of moral evil reflect self-deception rather than real intellectual difficulties. Our main task is to remove the mask from such self-deceptions and bring to the surface what people really know.

They will, of course, resist. They would rather remain in denial. That is why Naomi Wolf has recently been so roundly criticized by her fellow feminists. Like them, Miss Wolf is pro-abortion. The difference is that she has let the cat out of the bag. For years, she says, feminists have been pretending not to know that the fetus is a baby, but really they do know. For years they have been pretending not to know that abortion is murder, but really they know that. She forthrightly declares that abortion is real sin that incurs real guilt and requires real atonement, and that we have known it all along. The only problem is that Miss Wolf does not carry her reasoning to its conclusion. She wants women to go on aborting, but proposes that they hold candlelight vigils at abortion facilities afterward to show their sorrow. For Miss Wolf is pretending; she too is in denial. She pretends not to know that God is not mocked.

The paradox is that the natural law is both really known, and really suppressed. Among my Catholic friends, who see the knowledge, I stress the suppression; among my Reformed friends, who see the suppression, I stress the knowledge. Sometimes people think that suppressed moral knowledge is the same as *weakened* moral knowledge with weakened power over behavior. On the contrary, as we have seen in chapter two, pressing down one's conscience does not make it weak any more than pressing down a wildcat makes it docile. It only makes it violent. Its claws are even sharper in a culture with a Christian past, like ours, for then people have more to suppress. Our most secular institution still wraps itself in reminiscence of its past; the very tribunal which prohibits "endorsement" of God still opens its sessions with the words "God save the United States and this honorable Court." Hence the people of our generation must press down not only the present knowledge of general revelation, but also the troubling memory of special revelation. That is why they act so badly.

Our charge, then, is to find the ways to stir up that present knowledge and arouse that troubling memory. How?

STIRRING UP KNOWLEDGE AND MEMORY

We know how the knowledge and memory can be stirred and aroused in private conversation. One way is to *turn back the question*. A young man proclaimed "Morality is all relative anyway. How do we even know that murder is wrong?" My colleague asked him, "Are you at this moment in any real doubt about murder being wrong for everyone?" After a long uncomfortable silence the young man realized that he wasn't. My colleague replied simply, "Good. Then let's talk about something you really are in doubt about."

Another way is to *dissipate smoke*. A friend expressed dozens of objections to the point I was making about God; whenever I shot one down, he just deployed another. Recognizing that he was merely laying down a smoke barrage, I asked, "Suppose we took a few weeks and I answered every one of your objections to your complete intellectual satisfaction. Would you then believe?" He answered "No"— and that "No" was a moment of illumination, for he realized for the first time that his real problem with God was not in his mind, but in his will.

Some people are gifted in *connecting the dots*. A young woman went to pro-abortion meetings, chanted in a pro-abortion rally, and even gave a speech to a group of people about how her abortion had solved her crisis. Yet her burst of activism coincided with a suicidal depression known only to my friend, a college chaplain. She herself had invested too much in her happy-abortion story to suspect a link; he knew her well enough to suspect what the link might be. "If you hadn't had the abortion," he asked her, "when would the child have been born?" The answer was "Just about now." The wall of denial collapsed as she made the connection.

Still others are deft in *releasing the catch*. Asked whether they have suffered any emotional aftereffects from their abortions, most women say "No, I was fine." Abortion is never really "fine," but our culture does not like women to admit what their abortions really do to them—a point survey researchers tend to overlook. In speaking with post-abortive women, crisis pregnancy counselors seek to release the catch on the box of their hidden pain and guilt—not to force them to speak, but to give them permission. Often the catch reveals itself in what they say right after the obligatory statement that they were fine. Some say "No, I was fine, *but I'd never do it again,*" and the counselor can ask, "Why wouldn't you?" Others say "No, *other than the usual,*" and the counselor can ask, "What's the usual?"

Still another approach is to *play back the tape.* Many people are able to recognize their self-deceptions, if only they realize what they have actually been saying. All that is needed is to play back the tape, to hold up a mirror. I gently pointed out to one challenger that he had interrupted each one of my answers by asking another question from a different direction. Ordinarily a courteous fellow, he was abashed. "I guess I do," he said. "Why do I do that?" When I asked him why *he* thought he did, he frankly replied "I must not want to hear your answers." I merely suggested "Okay, then, let's talk about why you don't," and we were soon able to speak of what he really knew—but had been suppressing.

Yet another is *calling attention to the obvious.* Best, of course, is to get people to see it themselves by means of well-directed questions. For example, most abortion-minded women pretend to themselves that they are boxed in by circumstances; they say things like "I know abortion is wrong, but I just can't have a baby right now." One counselor I know simply asks, "What do you call what's in you?" Unless thoroughly drilled, hardly anyone calls it a "fetus"; no matter what her conscious views about abortion, almost every pregnant woman instinctively replies, "I call it a baby." But then my counselor friend can say without offense, "Then it sounds like you already have a baby. The question isn't whether to have one, but what you're going to do with the one you've got."

Then there is *tightening the noose*—bringing people to recognize the implications of their own choices. A great many modern people cling to the protection of views which are not merely false but incoherent; for instance, they dogmatically insist that truth cannot be known, all the while supposing that what they say is true. Once upon a time it was enough to point out the incoherency—to call attention to the obvious. No longer. Today the reply is likely to be, "I'm incoherent, but so what? I don't need coherency, and I can do without meaning." I answer, "I don't believe you, because we both know that the longing for meaning and coherency is deep-set in every mind, including yours. The real question, then, is this: What is it that is so important to you that you are willing to give up *even meaning, even coherency* to have it?"

A final way is to *do nothing, but wait for an opportunity from God.* An older, returning student confessed to me one day that my lecture about Aristotle had frightened him, and I saw that in very truth, he was shaking. All the pagan's talk about virtue had made him realize, he said, that he had not led a virtuous life. How interesting that God could use such an instrument to bring the conviction of sin.

In all these ways and more we can stir up the present knowledge of general revelation and arouse the troubling memory of special revelation, yet all of them are adapted to private conversation. The charge before us is to find ways to stir and arouse the same knowledge and memory in the public square. Not to succeed—that, thank God, is not our responsibility. But to try.

However it is to be done, the task is a matter of calling, of vocation. We are called to a political theory that assumes the moral law which no one else dares to avouch, and poses the questions which no one else dares to ask. We are called to a public apologetics that connects the dots of our nation's fragmented moral consciousness, and reminds people of what they know already. We are called to a civic rhetoric that dissipates smokescreens, and disperses self-deceptions. There are no such political theory, public apologetics, and civic rhetoric today. We are charged to found them.

The charge is too high for us, for we are a stunted generation. Even so, there is no one else to do it. If we neglect it, the next generation will be even shorter; if we lack the courage of our convictions, others will have the courage of their lack thereof. So let us try. Perhaps God will again choose "what is foolish in the world to shame the wise, ... what is weak in the world to shame the strong, ... what is low and despised in the world, even things that are not, to bring to nothing things that are, so that no human being might boast in the presence of God."

We are charged to be sustainers of this ever-perishing world, strewers of preserving salt, apostles of common grace. We are charged to prepare, by these lesser means, the way for the greater grace that saves: to make straight a highway for the King, Whose hem, but by grace, we are not fit to touch.

Index

Abortion
  and anoesis, 10
  and communitarianism, 77
  and complaisance, 129
  and expropriationism, 91;
  and guilt, 28-29, 33-34
  and moral decline, 20
  and neutralism, 100
  and post-abortion stress syndrome, 85
  and search for common ground, 138
  and traditionalism, 116
  as getting rid of the evidence, 32
  attempted justification for, 33-34
  contradictions in opinions concerning,
    26
  how to support young women
    tempted to commit, 124
  in scheme of book, 18
  in view of Naomi Wolf, 141
  knowledge of wrong of, 112
  middle cannot be right about, 65
  rate in cities, 136
  why committed, 125-135
  See also Knowledge and memory, ways
    to stir and arouse
Absolutionism. *See* Liberalism

Accommodation
  accommodationism, as hindrance to
    putting on the mind of Christ, 137-
    138
  mutual, among communities with re-
    lated stories, 86
  to sin, 128
  to wishes of others, 129
Achievement. *See* Problem of regime de-
  sign
Acres of Diamonds. See Conwell, Russell
Adams, John, his theory of balance of
  orders, 63
Affliction, John Donne's reflections on,
  133
After Virtue. See MacIntyre, Alasdair
Ambition, as a problem for filtration
  strategies, 60
Amenity, spoiled. *See* Motives and inten-
  tions
America a Christian Country. See Brewer,
  David
American Medical Association, proposal
  for organ harvesting, 21
Anapologetics. *See* Apologetics
Anna Karenina. See Tolstoy, Leo

Conservatism (cont.)
  kinds of, 107
  moral errors of
  civil religionism, 108-109
  instrumentalism, 72, 109-111
  moralism, 111-113
  Caesarism, 113-115
  traditionalism, 115-116
  neutralism, 117-119
  mammonism, 119-121
  meritism, 121-123
  problem with, 106-124
  See also Ideologies
Conwell, Russell, adherent of mammonism, 120
Cooley, Thomas, nineteenth-century jurist, adherent of instrumentalism, 110
Countervailing Vice, paradox of. *See* Paradox
Courage
  exemplifies virtue as a mean, 45
  illustrates unity of virtues, 47-48
Covenant
  Old and New, 72-74
  Zion, not America, the inheritor of, 109
Creation, reasoning backwards to, 80
Criteria, "external and overriding," 77-78
Cross, eyes lifted to, 105
Cue-taking, as legislative behavior, 62
Culture war, exactness of expression, 54
Cursus honorum ("course of honor," or progression through the magisterial ranks), 59
Custom, vicious, reason perverted by, 84

David, on witness of God's handiwork, 139
Debate, why proper, 41-42
DeLury, George E.
  his guilt over killing his wife, 26-28
  his possible motives for murder, 127
Denial. *See* Self-deception and denial
Depravity
  of conscience, 15
  of ideology, 84

of mind, 78
of nature, 4, 80
Design. *See* Witnesses
Desperate gestures. *See* Liberalism
Deterrence. *See* Problem of regime design
Diana of the Ephesians, whether an alternative to Jesus Christ, 13
Disease, venereal, 35
Displacement. *See* Conscience
Disposition of nature, evil, reason perverted by, 84
Dissipating smoke. *See* Knowledge and memory, ways to stir and arouse
Divorce. *See* Marriage
Doing nothing. *See* Knowledge and memory, ways to stir and arouse
Donne, John, his reflections on affliction, 133

Eastern Orthodoxy, possibilities for mutual accommodation, 86
Educational effects of public rules, 69
Eisenhower, Dwight David, adherent of civil religionism, 109
Elevation, paradox of. *See* Paradox
Elite, cultural, desires to suppress expression of belief in God, 39
Employment Division v. Smith (II), U.S. Supreme Court decision allowing "incidental" burden to religious practice, 114
Enlightenment, clinging to, 83
Epicureanism, noetic and apologetical, 7
Equality of concern and respect
  for rapist and victim, 9
  some as more equal than others, 94
Errors. *See* Fallacies
Establishment Clause (U.S. Constitution), and instrumentalism, 110
Etzioni, Amitai, spokesman for accountable communitarianism, 76
Euthanasia
  and moral decline, 20-21
  guilt of, 28-29
  in scheme of book, 18

A Note on the Author

J. BUDZISZEWSKI, a native of Milwaukee, holds a joint appointment in government and philosophy at the University of Texas, where he has taught since 1981. He holds his doctorate from Yale University. Dr. Budziszewski is the author of *Written on the Heart: The Case for Natural Law* and four other books. His articles have appeared in *First Things*, *National Review*, the *Journal of Politics*, and numerous other journals, and he writes a monthly column for *Boundless* webzine and *World* magazine.

This book was designed and set into type
by Mitchell S. Muncy,
and printed and bound
by Quebecor Printing Book Press
Brattleboro, Vermont.

❦

The text face is Caslon,
designed by Carol Twombly,
based on faces cut by William Caslon, London, in the 1730s
and issued in digital form by Adobe Systems,
Mountain View, California, in 1989.

❦

The cover illustration is *Expulsion from Paradise* by Michelangelo,
from the Sistine Chapel, Vatican Palace, Vatican State,
reproduced by agreement with Scala/Art Resource, New York, New York,
on a cover designed by Stephen J. Ott.

❦

The paper is acid-free and is of archival quality.

19